Jamaican Athletics

DEDICATED TO THE MEMORY OF BRENDA ROBINSON

HISTORIC RACE | Usain Bolt and Asafa Powell meet for the first time

The current and past Jamaican world record holders, Bolt and Powell, who are friends, stare down each other in an anticipated face off that fizzled at the Jamaica Olympic Trials 100m race on June 28, 2008. Bolt (*left*) was first; Michael Frater (*middle*), third and Asafa Powell (*right*), was second.

Jamaican Athletics

A MODEL FOR 2012 AND THE WORLD

Patrick Robinson

BlackAmber

BlackAmber, an imprint of
Arcadia Books Ltd
15-16 Nassau Street
London W1W 7AB
www.arcadiabooks.co.uk

First published in United Kingdom, 2009
Originally published in Jamaica, 3 impressions

A catalogue record for this book is available from the British Library

ISBN: 978-1-906413-30-9 (Hardcover)
ISBN: 978-1-906413-29-3 (Paperback)

Arcadia Books is the *Sunday Times* Small Publisher of the Year

Set in Adobe Garamond 13/20 x 33
Book and cover design by Neil Fairclough and Robert Harris
Printed in China by Regent Publishing Services

Contents

Reviews for Jamaican Athletics: A Model for the World

"This small treasure of a book by distinguished jurist Patrick Robinson is a feast for any fan who'd like to know more or be refreshed about Jamaican track & field: its history, the structure – including the national federation, the secondary schools sports association, the junior levels, etc., the CHAMPS (national HS championships), Coach Stephen Francis, junior and senior national records, international competition, etc. Color photos and small profiles of 24 champions are included."

Track and Field News, *2007.*

"The story of Jamaica's prowess in track and field arenas all over the world has been told over and over again. Not so well known though, is the background to this success. Why has Jamaica been able to produce exciting and world-beating talent year after year in athletics? What is the secret to the island's success, predominantly in sprint events, at the Olympic Games, International Association of Athletics Federations (IAAF) World Championships, Commonwealth Games, Pan American Games, Central American and Caribbean Games, World Junior Championships, World Youth Championships and the Carifta Games? In his book *Jamaican Athletics: A Model for the World,* first published in March 2007, Patrick Robinson answers these questions and more, in simple, but convincing style."

Elton Tucker, Jamaica Gleaner, *April 27, 2008.*

"I thought that one of its virtues was to point out the value to a nation of the efforts of its sportsmen and sportswomen, in this case its track and field athletes. The identification of champions with their tribe is as old as mankind. Every tribe should glory in the accomplishments of the victors and Arthur Lewis would say that it is the sign of the maturity of a society that it

Reviews for Jamaican Athletics: A Model for the World

recognizes and lauds it heroes. But one of the problems we face is having the medium and the message appropriate for the knowledge and recognition of heroes. This book serves to fill some of that space."

Sir George Alleyne, Chancellor of the University of the West Indies, Guest Speaker at the book signing in Washington, October 12, 2007.

"Allow me first of all to most warmly congratulate Patrick for this truly interesting and thought-provoking work . . . much of what Patrick writes in this book is of enduring significance . . . . His explanation of the mismatch between our first rate global rank in athletics and our relatively low rating in almost every other international ranking is insightful and thought provoking."

Professor Trevor Munroe, Guest speaker at the launch of Jamaican Athletics: A Model for the World, *Kingston, Jamaica, March 24, 2007.*

"Various explanations are offered in Robinson's rich analysis, . . . [as to why Jamaicans are strong in international athletics] . . . [b]ut the love and understanding shown by Judge Robinson for Jamaican athletics is outstanding."

Professor Stephen Vasciannie, article entitled "King of the Game", Daily Gleaner, *April 3, 2007.*

Jamaican Athletics: A Model for the World is a factual and insightful sketch of the wonderful tradition of Jamaican athletics of which 'Champs' is an integral part. . . . Justice Robinson has created time in his busy schedule to open many eyes to our world class act by putting the case in true perspective which we knew but never tied down. . . .

Mark Loague, "A Century Beckons", Boys and Girls Athletic Championships Magazine, 2007.

Foreword

JAMAICAN ATHLETES HAVE PERFORMED WITH distinction at the highest international level for many years. The experience and results at the Games of the XXIX Olympiad in Beijing, China in 2008 were truly exceptional and raised the bar considerably on our already existing high standards. The Beijing chapter in the book captures the remarkable achievements of our athletes and validates clearly the claims in the author's previous work, *Jamaican Athletics: A Model for the World*, which gave more than a hint of the potential that was realized at the Games.

This book documents clearly the success story of Jamaican athletics particularly since we first competed in the 1948 Olympic Games in London and it also presents insights into the support systems that have contributed to this success. Due recognition has been given to the outstanding coaches and mentors who perhaps have not been properly recognized over the years and readers will have a better understanding of the various elements, including the structure and system that are the critical components of the athletic landscape in Jamaica. The material contained in this publication will undoubtedly be of great value to all who are interested in this sport as well as others who are fascinated by this Jamaican phenomenon.

The author Patrick Robinson has done his research well and because of his personal interest and passion for athletics and sport generally has been able to combine statistics with human and social insights to present this extremely valuable publication. I commend this publication to all and congratulate the author for an excellent book.

Hon. Michael S. Fennell, OJ, CD, President, Jamaica Olympic Association
President, Commonwealth Games Federation

Preface

CONSIDERING JAMAICA'S PRE-EMINENCE IN GLOBAL ATHLETICS – a position that is wholly disproportionate to its size and resources – it is only right that there should be an analysis of the environment in which what the author calls "the athletic product of excellence" thrives. For athletes do not produce themselves; rather, they are the product of a system, and the degree of success that they achieve is directly proportionate to the effectiveness of that system.

Jamaican Athletics: A Model for 2012 and the World presents this analysis, and, in my view, it is necessary. For, as the book explains, it is important that we know why Jamaica had a McKenley, a Quarrie, an Ottey, and today has a Powell, a Bolt and a Campbell-Brown so that we are in the best position to ensure the recreation of the qualities that produced those great athletes.

The book has many themes. But there are two that are important, not only for Jamaican athletics, but for Jamaica as a whole.

The first is excellence. Track and field athletics is described as "arguably, the highest quality Jamaican product of international standard – a veritable oasis of excellence." The Jamaica Amateur Athletic Association, which is responsible for the development of athletics and the promotion and organization of athletic meetings in Jamaica, is proud to be part of an enterprise that has been lauded in such terms. The heights of excellence attained in athletics are achievable by any Jamaican individual or enterprise.

That brings me to the second theme, the talent and capability of Jamaicans. In praising the work of the two great coaches, Stephen Francis and Glen Mills, the author says "By their example of self-confidence, self-reliance, dedication to task and the application of the highest professional standards, they have demonstrated that Jamaicans can, to echo the rallying cry of Marcus Garvey, accomplish what they will." The message is clear. We are justifiably proud of our athletic achievements over the past six decades, and particularly, of those at the Beijing Olympic Games. But if we want to ensure that Jamaica remains at the pinnacle of global athletics, we must find the will, the means and the solidarity that will enable us to create and implement the programmes necessary to accomplish that task.

HOWARD ARIS
President, Jamaica Amateur Athletics Association

Acknowledgements

I MUST ACKNOWLEDGE THE CONTINUED support of Laurie Foster in ensuring that the data in the book is correct and for providing the vast majority of captions for the photographs.

Special thanks to Kim Hoo Fatt for doing the proof reading/editorial work and Kellie Magnus for general advice. Special thanks to Judith Robinson, Brando Hayden, Quam Byll-Cataria, veteran coach Glen Mills, Basil Benjie of the Jamaica Teachers' Association, Charlie Fuller, and to Yannis Pitsiladis for information on genetic research. I apologise to Charlie Fuller for the incorrect citation of his name and to Dennis Johnson for the incorrect naming of his school, in the third edition of *Jamaican Athletics: A Model for the World*.

Michael Prescod's help in the design and formulation of the introductory paragraphs of the chapter on the Beijing Olympics is also acknowledged.

Photographs were obtained from Getty Images, Sporting Heroes, Jamaica Observer, the Associated Press and Anthony Foster.

I must also express my gratitude to my secretary Margaret McCutcheon for her assistance in the production of the book and to Janice Looman-Kearns and Frances Walsh for general assistance.

Usain Bolt

Jamaican Athletics

A MODEL FOR 2012 AND THE WORLD

ARTHUR WINT

Jamaica's first Olympic Gold Medallist – 400m, London 1948.

I. *Introduction*

IN AN ADDRESS IN KINGSTON, JAMAICA on November 4, 2006, Count Jacques Rogge, President of the International Olympic Committee (IOC), lauded Jamaica's achievements at the Olympic Games, commenting that this success was not achieved by accident, but resulted from "a good system to prepare athletes". He referred to the great respect that the IOC had for Jamaica and also remarked that, for a population of less than three million, Jamaica's achievement was "really outstanding". Since 1948 Jamaica has won 13 gold, 27 silver and 21 bronze medals at the Olympic Games.[1]

Jamaica has also won 7 gold, 29 silver and 30 bronze medals at the World Championships.

At recent Olympic Games and World Championships, Jamaica's track and field teams have placed in the top ten, and on occasions have won more medals than the United

DONALD QUARRIE ▶

His stunningly effective bend sprinting was the feature of his many furlong victories, including the Olympic title in Montreal, 1976, and medals on several relay teams at major events.

3

JAMAICA COLLEGE TRACK TEAM – 1911

Norman Manley, (*second left, middle row*) the forerunner of all the great Jamaican athletes. He is shown here with the Jamaica College track team that won CHAMPS in 1911. His achievement of winning six events at CHAMPS has never been equalled. His record run of 10 seconds for the 100 yards was not broken until 1952, and his time in the 220 yards would have put him in the final of that event at both the 1908 and 1912 Olympic Games. Norman Manley later became Premier of Jamaica and is a National Hero.

Kingdom. Considering the difference in population and resources – the UK has a population of 60 million and its athletes are funded by national lottery money – this is remarkable. At several stagings of the International Association of Athletics Federation (IAAF) World Junior Championships in Athletics, Jamaica has finished in the top ten. To place in such a position in any activity of a genuinely global character, such as track and field athletics, would be a significant achievement for any country, but for Jamaica it is even more noteworthy in light of its size and limited resources. At the 2006 Commonwealth Games held in Melbourne, Jamaica was second only to host country Australia in athletics. In winning all the sprint events – 100 metres, 200 metres, sprint hurdles and 4x100 metres relay, for men and women – at those Games, Jamaica became only the third country in modern athletics (the others being Australia, in the 1950 Auckland Commonwealth Games and the USA at the 1984 Los Angeles Olympics) to complete a sweep of all sprint events at a major athletic championship (Olympics, World Championships or Commonwealth Games).

At the 2007 Osaka World Championships, from a field of 204 countries Jamaica, with ten medals, placed fourth in the overall medal count.

At the 2008 Beijing Olympics, from a field of 204 countries Jamaica, with 11 medals, placed third in the overall medal count.

RAYMOND STEWART

Airborne, seen at a US Collegiate meet sprinting away from world class athletes, Frankie Fredericks, Andre Cason and Mike Marsh. Stewart placed sixth in the 1984 Los Angeles 100m at age 19, a few months after leaving Camperdown High School.

In the Commonwealth Caribbean, Jamaica is at the top of the table in athletics, and in the wider Latin American and North American area it is only the USA, and perhaps, Cuba that are ahead of Jamaica. The world record holder in the men's 100 metres (Usain Bolt); the former world record holder (Asafa Powell); the world record holder in the men's 200 metres (Usain Bolt); the gold medallist in the women's 100 metres at the 2007 Osaka World Championships as well as the 200 metres at the 2008 Beijing Olympic Games (Veronica Campbell-Brown); the gold medallist in the women's 100 metres at the 2008 Beijing Olympic Games (Shelly-Ann Fraser); the gold medallist in the women's 400 metres hurdles and Olympic record holder at the Beijing Olympic Games (Melaine Walker) and the 2006 world-ranked number 1 in the women's 100 and 200 metres (Sherone Simpson), are all Jamaicans. Asafa Powell was named World Male Athlete for 2006 by the IAAF.

In the television coverage in the USA of the 2007 World Championships one grew tired of hearing commentators saying, "so it's Jamaica vs USA again". What is it that allowed or obliged the commentators to frame the issue this way? What is it that explains why in a truly global event among 204 countries it came down time and

MARILYN NEUFVILLE ▶

She set a 400m World Record – 51.02 – at the Edinburgh Commonwealth Games at the tender age of 17.

BERTLAND CAMERON

Bert Cameron created history by winning Jamaica's first World Championships Gold Medal in taking the 400m at the inaugural event in Helsinki (1983).

again to a contest between the USA and Jamaica? The question is very much warranted. After all, the difference in size and resources of the two countries is of David and Goliath proportions. A country with a population of less than 3 million and with far fewer resources (per capita income of US$4,600), takes on a giant of a country with a population of 300 million and far greater resources (per capita income of US$35,000), and is its equal or better on many occasions. Moreover, the 2007 World Championships was not the first time; since 1948 Jamaica has consistently been a challenger to the USA and many other bigger and much better resourced countries in global track and field athletics.

The book, therefore, in large measure, seeks to provide an explanation as to how there can be a contest, and a legitimate one at that, between Jamaica and a country like the USA, not relating to conduct that has negative and anti-social implications (such as, which country has the higher number of murders and gun crimes on a per capita basis), but rather, an activity that is positive and meaningful for both countries.

JULIET CAMPBELL ▶

A very long and magnificent service to Jamaica, in the 200m and 400m events, highlighted by a 200m gold at the 2001 Lisbon World Indoor Championships and back to back Commonwealth silver in Kuala Lumpur in 1998 and Manchester in 2002.

MERLENE OTTEY

Her longevity spoke volumes
for true grit and determination;
her 28 medals at the highest
level, an awesome challenge for
any future athlete.

Count Rogge is right. Jamaica's success in track and field athletics is not fortuitous; it is the result of a system of athletic instruction, management and administration that has been in place, tried and tested for almost a hundred years, and is now well established. There is no activity or area of endeavour in Jamaica whether in the public or private sector that, operating at a national level, is as well organized and, applying international standards, has been as consistently successful as track and field athletics. It is, arguably, the highest quality Jamaican product of international standard – a veritable oasis of excellence. Other areas of enterprise in Jamaica would do well to study this phenomenon with a view to ascertaining how this level of success has been achieved in a country plagued with so many problems that are said to be antithetical to growth and development. What are the features of this system that have consistently been at work over the years to create a product of which every Jamaican can be justly proud, and which is the envy of many advanced and developed countries? Can the practices in track and field athletics be emulated and used to our advantage in other areas of national life?

▶ Did you know?

At the 1948 London Olympics and the 1952 Helsinki Olympics, Jamaica placed third in the medal tables in track and field athletics.

Seen here (536) taking the 100m silver medal at the 1968 Mexico City Olympics. Winner is Jim Hines (USA-279).

2. *Foundations of the System*

THE ANNUAL INTERSCHOLASTIC CHAMPIONSHIPS (called "CHAMPS" by every Jamaican) is at the heart of the system of which I speak. It was started in 1910 and, in the following year, produced in Norman Manley an athlete of the highest quality. Having broken the 100 yards record with a run of 10 seconds at a time when the world best was 9.7 seconds, and having run 23 seconds for the 220 yards – the latter, a time that would have placed him in the final of that event at both the 1908 and 1912 Olympics – it is clear that, had he chosen an athletic career, Norman Manley would have been very competitive at the international level. Thus Jamaica was producing athletes of international calibre from almost 100 years ago, but may not have known it!

Later, Norman Manley was to win a Rhodes Scholarship and was awarded a Military Medal for bravery in the First World War. He was also to become a distinguished

DEON HEMMINGS ▶
Her 400m hurdles triumph in Atlanta 1996 was the first Olympic Gold Medal won by a female from the English-speaking Caribbean.

GRACE JACKSON

Seen winning on the US
Indoor Circuit. Her 21.72
national record for the 200m
silver medal at the 1988
Seoul Games provided the
high point of her career
which spanned three
Olympics.

barrister throughout the Commonwealth, one of the founding fathers of Jamaica's independence, Premier of Jamaica, and a National Hero. One must also mention from that era, G.C. Foster (after whom Jamaica's only Sports College is named), who was a sprinter of international calibre, and who became a legendary coach with an uncanny knack for identifying students who turned out to be good athletes.

But the real significance of Norman Manley's achievements is that he established a standard of athletic excellence in schools, that was followed in the late 1930s and early 1940s by others, notably Arthur Wint, Douglas Manley (who equalled the 100 yards record of his father, Norman), Leroy 'Coco' Brown and Herb McKenley. At its first and second Olympics in 1948 and 1952, Jamaica – still a colony of the UK – won three gold and five silver medals, including the world record breaking 4x400 metres relay, in which it defeated the USA. The exploits of Arthur Wint, Herb McKenley, George Rhoden and Les Laing at those Olympics signalled to the world that Jamaica was a country blessed with immense talent in athletics. Tribute must also be paid to their contemporaries, Cynthia Thompson, Vinton Beckett, Kathleen Russell and Carmen

LES LAING ▶

A valiant athlete who represented Jamaica with distinction in the 1940s and 1950s, and was a member of the record breaking team in the 4x400m relay at the 1952 Helsinki Olympics.

The British West Indies Bronze Medal winning 4x400m relay team, with three Jamaicans at right of photo, seen on the podium after the medal ceremony at the Rome 1960 Olympics. From left *(sitting)* Keith Gardner, George Kerr; *(standing)* Mal Spence and Jim Wedderburn (BAR).

Phipps, who must be seen as the forerunners of Jamaica's dominant female athletes from the 1980s to the present. From that time no decade passed in which Jamaica did not produce athletes of the highest calibre. Note may be taken of Keith Gardner, the twins, Mal and Mel Spence, Una Morris, George Kerr, Dennis Johnson and Lennox Miller. Errol Stewart, Michael Fray, Clifton Forbes and Miller himself broke the 4x100 metres relay world record in the heats and again in the semi-final at the 1968 Mexico City Olympics, and subsequently placed fourth in the final. There also have been Marilyn Neufville, Donald Quarrie, Seymour Newman, Raymond Stewart, Bertland Cameron, Merlene Ottey, Juliet Cuthbert, Grace Jackson, Winthrop Graham, Gregory Haughton, Roxbert Martin, Davian Clarke, Michelle Freeman, Deon Hemmings, Sandie Richards, Lorraine Graham-Fenton, Tayna Lawrence, and of course the current crop – Usain Bolt, Asafa Powell, Veronica Campbell-Brown, Sherone Simpson, Shelly-Ann Fraser, Melaine Walker, Kerron Stewart, Nesta Carter, Marvin Anderson, James Beckford, Michael Frater, Shericka Williams, Novelene Williams, Danny McFarlane, Maurice Wignall and Trecia-Kaye Smith.

The significance of this list[2], which is not exhaustive, is that it points to a tradition of excellence in athletics that can be matched by no more than ten other countries. Thus over the past nine and a half decades young Jamaican athletes and Jamaicans as a whole

THE MAGNIFICENT FOUR ▶

From left to right, George Rhoden, Les Laing, Arthur Wint and Herb McKenley. Their record breaking run in the 4x400m relay at the 1952 Helsinki Olympic Games will forever inspire other Jamaican athletes.

GEORGE RHODEN

A world class 400m runner in the 1940s and 1950s. He ran superbly in the final leg of the 4x400m relay in which Jamaica won the gold medal at the 1952 Helsinki Olympic Games. He is shown here at far left winning the gold medal in the 400m at the same Games; in lane 5 is Herb McKenley (silver medal) and in lane 3 is Arthur Wint (5th place).

have always had heroes and heroines in athletics, to admire and emulate. The value of role models in any field of human endeavour is not to be underestimated. It would be difficult for a youngster not to be inspired by McKenley's magnificent 44.6 seconds third leg in the 4x400 metres relay at Helsinki when he made up a deficit of more than 15 metres, thereby ultimately ensuring Jamaica's historic victory.

Many calculations have been made over the years to compare McKenley's time to the performance of today's athletes; all of these calculations have the same result: they show that his time of 44.6 seconds on a cinder track, in contrast to the modern and faster synthetic surface, must rank as one of the greatest 400 metres ever run in any era.

The current crop of Jamaican athletes, including Asafa Powell, Veronica Campbell-Brown and Usain Bolt had Merlene Ottey, Juliet Cuthbert and Grace Jackson to emulate; those three had Don Quarrie and Bertland Cameron, who had Lennox Miller, who had Dennis Johnson. Of course, every athlete after 1952 had the great relay quartet of Arthur Wint, Herb McKenley, George Rhoden and Les Laing, and those four would have been inspired by Norman Manley.

This long unbroken line of high calibre Jamaican athletes has ensured that every generation of athletes has always had a role model and hero or heroine as inspiration – a factor that undoubtedly is a large part of the explanation for our success.

> ## Did you know?

Usain Bolt holds the World Record in the 100 metres, 9.69 seconds, the World Junior Record and the World Youth Record in the 200 metres. Bolt also has the distinction of being the youngest champion ever in the World Junior Championships, winning the 200 metres in Kingston in 2002 at the tender age of 15. At the Jamaican National Championships (June 22–24, 2007), Bolt broke Donald Quarrie's 36-year-old national record of 19.86 seconds for the 200 metres with a time of 19.75 seconds. He now holds the World Record in the 200 metres with a time of 19.30 seconds.

DONALD QUARRIE

Five time Olympian, Donald Quarrie (451), taking second here in a 100m heat at the 1980 Moscow Olympics. Quarrie won gold (200m, Montreal '76), silver (100m, Montreal '76), bronze (200m, Moscow '80) and silver (4x100m, Los Angeles '84).

An essay on the explanation of Jamaica's pre-eminence in global athletics would be open to criticism if it did not say something about the Jamaican personality, which is well known for its competitiveness, its assertiveness and its self-confidence. One mentions these attributes even if one is not able to explain why, if they contribute to success in track and field athletics, they do not, or do not appear to have the same effect in other areas of national life.

Edward Seaga, former Prime Minister of Jamaica and a sociologist, contends that the environment of scarcity and lack of space in which inner-city children live has produced a "determination to aggressively and competitively overcome the odds of scarcity with challenging responses".[3] Of course, he was not seeking to explain Jamaica's pre-eminence in global athletics, and I do not know how many of our athletes are from the inner city.[4] But that information is not necessary to warrant the conclusion that, in a country with a per capita income of US$4,600 and a high rate of unemployment, youngsters with talent will find the opportunities for economic advancement presented by athletics attractive and, perhaps, even irresistible. For, in those circumstances, scarcity and the hunger for economic betterment are not confined to the inner city.

MARVIN ANDERSON ▶

An outstanding sprinter at the high school level, Anderson, under new coach Raymond Stewart, placed 6th in the 200m at the Osaka World Championships.

ARTHUR WINT

Arthur Wint (22) wins Jamaica's first Olympic Gold in the 1948 London Games ahead of his countryman Herb McKenley (90).

Competitiveness, combativeness and assertiveness (some might say this is a euphemism for aggressiveness, but I believe the more accurate description is assertiveness) are an integral part of the Jamaican persona and identity. Indeed, there are some legendary stories of Jamaicans abroad standing up for themselves and others against brute force and injustice. It is well known that in London in the 1960s Jamaicans had such a reputation for defending themselves against racist skinheads that many persons from other Caribbean countries and even from Africa indentified themselves as Jamaicans in order to forestall such attacks.

What does all this have to do with Jamaica's consistently high ranking in global athletics? The cynic might say, arguably, everything or nothing. But I maintain that the innate Jamaican spirit, self-assurance and self-belief are relevant factors in a search for the explanation of Jamaica's success in athletics. I give two examples.

In the semi-finals of the 400 metres at the 1984 Los Angeles Olympics, Bertland Cameron, who was a favourite for the gold medal, pulled a hamstring muscle at about 110 metres, hopped for some 40 metres, losing about 10 metres to his rivals, but did not stop as most runners in the same situation would have done. He continued and, in one of the most astonishing displays of bravery and resilience ever seen at the

▶ Did you know?

Jamaica performed superbly at its first two Olympic Games. At the 1948 London Olympics, Arthur Wint was the gold and silver medallist in the 400 and 800 metres, respectively, while Herb McKenley was second to his compatriot in the 400 metres. At the 1952 Helsinki Olympics, George Rhoden won the gold medal in the 400 metres; Herb McKenley was the silver medallist in the same event as well as the 100 metres; Arthur Wint won a silver medal in the 800 metres, and those three, along with Les Laing, were gold medallists in the 4x400 metres relay in the world record time of 3:03.9 seconds.

DENNIS JOHNSON

Phenomenal school boy sprinter for Calabar High School, who, under the guidance of the great American coach Bud Winter, equalled the 100 yards record on four occasions in a period of six weeks in 1961. He was for decades a successful coach at the College of Arts, Science and Technology (later the University of Technology), where his coaching and training regimen laid the foundation for the modern adult athletic programme in Jamaica.

Olympics, finished the race qualifying in fourth place with a time of 45.10 seconds.[5] Many believe that had he not been injured, Bertland would have broken the then world record of 43.86 seconds.

The other example is taken from the final of the 400 metres relay at the 1996 Atlanta Olympics, when at the final baton change Gregory Haughton fell to the ground. His reaction was not to surrender; instead, he instinctively executed a somersault that would have been the envy of many Olympic gymnasts, got to his feet and brought home a bronze medal for his country. It would be difficult to give a better example of the "never say die" attitude and the self-belief that typify Jamaicans.

The role that Jamaica's sucess in global athletics has played in fostering national pride cannot be overstressed. The fact that this success has been sustained over such a long period gives added significance to this role. Every country needs its heroes and role models for inspiration and emulation, and to promote national pride. We are very fortunate in Jamaica that athletics has for a very long time been such a legitimate and reliable example of excellence at the international level. In no small measure that success has served to promote individual and national self-esteem; the self-confidence that comes from that process is instilled in the psyche of every Jamaican, and there can be no doubt that this is evident in the self-belief that characterizes our athletes.

▶ Did you know?

The second, and perhaps the most important feature of the system, is the rigour of the training regimen that prepares the athletes for CHAMPS. Here, the difference in eras is very marked. Forty to fifty years ago boys were little more than "gentlemen" athletes, who started training in January for CHAMPS in April. Today's athletes start training in September of the previous year for CHAMPS in March or April of the succeeding year. In some cases, they start from June or July, that is, a full nine or ten months before CHAMPS.

JULIET CUTHBERT

Silver medals (100m, 200m) at the Barcelona Olympics; 1992 proved to be the highlight of a long career which spanned five Olympics.

This, then – a rich athletic history and tradition, supported by the assertiveness, the combativeness, the self-belief and resilience that are native to the Jamaican persona – is the first explanation of Jamaica's success. These are factors that contribute to and facilitate the operation of the system that is the foundation for our success in track and field athletics.

Another contributory factor is the prodigious athletic talent in Jamaica. However, without the system that is in place to nurture it, the natural talent could not produce the results we have today. Many other countries have natural athletic talent. But, lacking the Jamaican system, their results are not as consistently good as ours. It must be acknowledged, however, that among the Commonwealth Caribbean countries, The Bahamas, and Trinidad and Tobago also perform very well.

It has long been claimed that black people of the West African diaspora (to which the vast majority of Jamaicans belong) are genetically predisposed to excellence in sports that call for explosive talent. In track the explosive events are the 100, 200 and 400 metres as well as the hurdles and the jumps. A Jamaican journalist, Patrick

VERONICA CAMPBELL-BROWN ▶

She has garnered at the international level a treasure trove of medals, unmatched in quantity and quality by any other Jamaican. Here she shows her delight in winning the gold medal in the 100m at the 2007 Osaka World Championships.

ASAFA POWELL

2006 SPRINT KING

Anchoring the men's sprint relay team to victory at the Commonwealth Games (Melbourne, 2006). Powell went on to equal his 100m World Record (9.77) twice during the season and to break his own record with a time of 9.74 seconds on September 9, 2007.

Cooper, in his book *The Black Superman*[6], advances the thesis that there is a scientific basis for the dominance of blacks of the West African diaspora in explosive sports such as athletics, basketball, baseball, football, American football, boxing and cricket. To his credit Cooper anticipates the objection that his thesis feeds into the stereotype of blacks as people with brawn and no brains; he, therefore, takes care to highlight the many achievements of blacks in areas outside the field of sports, and identifies the social and political factors explaining their relative underachievement in those areas.

Important research into the genetic determinants of physical performance is being carried out by the University of Glasgow through its new Research Centre, The International Centre for East African Running Science (www.icears.org). This project has active partners in more than 14 countries, including the University of the West Indies in Kingston, Jamaica.

In 2002 ICEARS scientists carried out two studies examining whether the genotype distribution in Ethiopian and Kenyan endurance athletics differed significantly from that of their respective general populations. Despite the speculation

MICHAEL FRATER ▶
A 100m silver medal at the 2005 Helsinki World Championships demonstrated the depth of Jamaican male sprinting.

GREGORY HAUGHTON

With a succession of individual and mile relay medals at the highest level, Haughton is most remembered for his "kinpupalik"*, recovering from a fall after receiving the baton on the final leg of the mile relay at the Atlanta Olmypics – a true testimony to Jamaican resilience, resourcefulness and "never-say-die" attitude.

* Jamaican dialect for somersault

that African athletes have a genetic advantage, no genetic evidence was found to suggest that this is the case, although research is at the early stage.[7]

More recently, ICEARS scientists sampled over 500 of the world's best sprinters from the USA, Nigeria and Jamaica, and are currently completing the initial genetic analysis.[8]

ICEARS scientists are testing the hypothesis that the Jamaican "sprint factory" phenomenon may be due to the eugenic effects of the slave trade, that is, only the fittest were selected from West Africa as slaves and only the toughest survived the journey and slavery. The hypothesis that the East African dominance of distance running may be due to a positive natural selection to high altitude is also being examined.

Edward Seaga points to environmental factors that may account for Jamaica's excellence in sports. He refers to studies showing that "permissive child-rearing practices often result in motor precocity, or in other words, superior muscular coordination".[9]

TAYNA LAWRENCE ▶

Will always be remembered for her surprise 100m bronze medal at the Sydney Olympics in 2000. Persistent injury cut her career short in 2006.

The following tribute was paid to Arthur Wint by the author at the book signing in Toronto on November 1, 2007, and inscribed in a copy of *Jamaican Athletics: A Model for the World*[10] presented to his daughter.

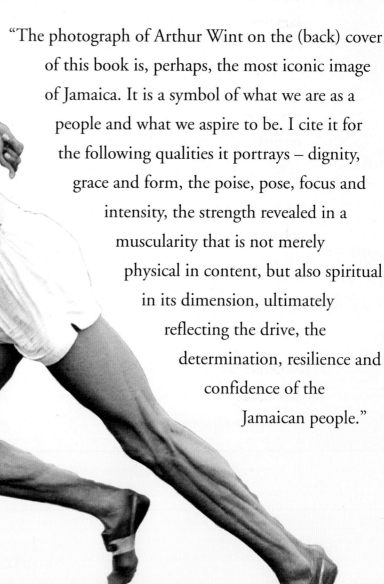

"The photograph of Arthur Wint on the (back) cover of this book is, perhaps, the most iconic image of Jamaica. It is a symbol of what we are as a people and what we aspire to be. I cite it for the following qualities it portrays – dignity, grace and form, the poise, pose, focus and intensity, the strength revealed in a muscularity that is not merely physical in content, but also spiritual in its dimension, ultimately reflecting the drive, the determination, resilience and confidence of the Jamaican people."

In examining the factors accounting for Jamaica's success in global athletics, one cannot help but notice that many of the athletes who have represented Jamaica, including some who have excelled at the international level, come from Trelawny, one of the 14 parishes in Jamaica. This list includes Usain Bolt, Veronica Campbell-Brown and George Kerr. Ben Johnson who represented Canada in the 100 metres is also from the parish of Trelawny.

Anecdotal evidence is that Trelawny yams are of exceptionally high nutritional value, and it is popularly believed that this explains why the parish produces such great athletes.

In its genetic analysis of Jamaican sprinters, ICEARS is conducting studies relating to a number of Jamaican athletes, a number of persons representative of the Jamaican population and a number of persons from the parish of Trelawny.

A list of the great Trelawny athletes is set out in Annex II.

Whether there are genetic or environmental factors accounting for or contributing to Jamaica's success in global athletics, it is very evident that there abounds in Jamaica tremendous talent in athletics, particularly in the sprints, hurdles and jumps. This talent is available for the system to develop.

▶ Did you know?

In 1910 there were six secondary schools and, perhaps, no more than 70 athletes competing at CHAMPS. At CHAMPS in the present era some 85 Boys' and 70 Girls' schools and about 2,200 athletes (1,280 boys and 920 girls) participate. The Meet takes place at the National Stadium over a period of four days. It attracts the attention of every Jamaican, and there is scarcely another event in Jamaica that is as popular.

TRIBUTE TO THE HONOURABLE

The following tribute was paid to Herb McKenley by the author, presented to his widow and daughters at the signing of the book *Jamaican Athletics: A Model for the World* at the Lexington Hotel, Orlando, Florida, January 4, 2008, and to his son at the signing of the book in Atlanta on May 3, 2008.

AMONG THE FACTORS THAT EXPLAIN JAMAICA'S phenomenal and consistent success in international athletics are the country's rich tradition in that sport and the extent and quality of the coaching in schools. No one has made a greater contribution to that tradition and to the training of our athletes than the late Herbert McKenley.

Any history of modern international athletics will be obliged to record its indebtedness to Herb (as he was affectionately called) for converting the 400 metres into a sprint event. And Jamaica will always be grateful to Herb not only for his athletic excellence, but more importantly, for the example of perseverance offered by his career as an athlete. If in these troubled times in our country, it is desired to illustrate, particularly to young people, how determination and resilience can transform disappointment into challenge and hope, and ultimately into success, Herb's career is the perfect model.

Despite the fame and greatness achieved by Mr. Mc

(another name by which he was affectionately known), he remained humble and approachable to all throughout his life. These traits carried over naturally into his long and distinguished coaching career, in which he exhibited a concern not only for his charges' athletic potential, but also for their overall development as persons.

Like all great coaches, he imparted not only technical knowledge; he was in essence a teacher and a motivator. No tribute to Herb would be complete without placing on record Jamaica's gratitude for the hundreds of athletic scholarships – one count puts the number at almost a thousand – he secured for our students at colleges and universities in the USA.

It is not without significance that, although the book being signed this evening is not so much about great Jamaican athletes as it is about isolating the environment in which that culture of greatness thrives, the following two paragraphs are devoted to Herb.

HERB McKENLEY OM, OJ, CD

"... thus over the past nine and a half decades young Jamaican athletes and Jamaicans as a whole have always had heroes and heroines in athletics, to admire and emulate. The value of role models in any field of human endeavour is not to be underestimated. It would be difficult for a youngster not to be inspired by McKenley's magnificent 44.6 seconds third leg in the 4x400 metres relay at Helsinki when he made up a deficit of more than 15 metres, thereby ultimately ensuring Jamaica's historic victory.

Many calculations have been made over the years to compare McKenley's time to the performance of today's athletes; all of these calculations have the same result: they show that his time of 44.6 seconds on a cinder track, in contrast to the modern and faster synthetic surface, must rank as one of the greatest 400 metres ever run in any era."

In a nutshell, these lines tell the story of the Honourable Herbert McKenley, OM, OJ, CD, the athlete and the man.

35

BRIGITTE FOSTER-HYLTON

A pioneer of the "stay at home" training regime of super coach Stephen Francis, she won silver and bronze 100m hurdles medals at the 2003 Paris and 2005 Helsinki World Championships, respectively.

3. *The Structure of the System*

▸ Did you know?

Years ago there were two or three development meets prior to CHAMPS. In the present era in the JAAA's Calendar of Events there are typically listed about 27 preparatory and development meets prior to CHAMPS. Although there are so many meets in the relatively short period of four months, they are not treated casually by schools, coaches and athletes. They are taken very seriously.

THE SYSTEM CONSISTS OF A STRUCTURE with a number of relatively disparate actors. There is the Jamaica Olympic Association (JOA), the conduit to the Olympic Movement; the Jamaica Amateur Athletic Association (JAAA), which has among its functions the development of amateur athletics and the promotion and organization of athletic meetings in Jamaica; the Jamaica Teachers' Association, which organizes the district and parish meets as well as the National Championships for the primary, all age and junior high schools; the primary, all age and junior high schools; the Inter Secondary School Sports Association (ISSA), which is responsible for organizing and managing the sports programme in the secondary schools; the secondary schools, their principals, their coaches, and supporters, comprising mainly alumni, especially at the secondary level; the G.C. Foster College of Physical Education and Sport (the G.C. Foster College); the University of Technology (UTech); the Coaches at the tertiary or adult level; the Ministry with responsibility for sports; the Ministry of Education; the Jamaica Defence Force, which provides logistical and other support for track meets; and the private sector, which is increasingly becoming engaged in the system.

Although the JAAA, the ISSA and the Ministry have functions and powers that can impact on other actors, I do not see the system as being hierarchical or overly centralized; there is no single actor with authority to control the other actors. This conclusion in no way detracts from the important general policy-making roles of the JAAA, the ISSA and the Ministry.

The system operates at a level of organization that allows each actor a certain space and flexibility in his sphere. The question may be asked, why, despite this looseness, it is successful. The answer is that in some systems a structure that is not rigidly centralized, but is more relaxed in the way it shapes the relationship between its actors, is a virtue, not a disadvantage, so long as each actor understands well his role and is willing to discharge it to the best of his ability. Individual expression and the attainment of high standards are facilitated, not thwarted, by this lack of rigidity or looseness. Moreover, in contradistinction to the relative looseness of the system as a whole, the subsystem of each actor is run very tightly from its centre.

It may also be remarked that other sports in Jamaica, such as cricket and football, have, roughly, the same structure – a national body, schools, coaches, alumni, the ISSA, the relevant ministry and the private sector – as track and field athletics, and yet do not achieve anything remotely close to its success at either the local, regional or international level. The popular explanation for this disparity is that, whereas most of those activities are team sports, track and field athletics is, except for the relays, an individual sport.

4. *Features of the System*

PRE-SECONDARY LEVEL

ALTHOUGH THE ENGINE THAT DRIVES JAMAICA'S success in athletics is the athletic programme in its secondary schools, the primary, all age and junior high schools play an important role in exposing youngsters to the sport at an early age.

The Jamaica Teachers' Association has built an intricate organization for its athletic programme in primary, all age and junior high schools at school, district, parish and national level. Each school has its own meet with inter-house competition; from these meets athletes are identified to represent schools at the district level. From competitions at the 76 district levels, athletes vie for selection to the parish teams. Finally, the 14 parishes compete at the National Primary, All Age and Junior High Schools Athletic Championships held annually at the National Stadium – a meet that attracts over 1,200 participants.

When the first All Island Primary and All Age Schools Sports was held in 1962, Sir Alexander Bustamante, the Premier of Jamaica, said "it is the best thing that has happened to Primary and All Age Schools in living memory." While that assessment

4X100m WOMEN'S RELAY FINAL

Jamaica, with Veronica Campbell on anchor taking the country's first sprint relay gold medal ever at the 2004 Athens Olympics.

40

may be open to debate, what is beyond question is the value of the meet and the tremendous contribution it has made to Jamaican athletics. The National Championships has been described as a nursery – "a nurturing ground for junior athletes". It is at this meet that talent is recognized and athletes are recruited by secondary school coaches. Of course, it is at the secondary schools where, with better coaching, better training facilities and better nutrition, the potential of these young athletes is developed in a programme that is second to none in the world.

But secondary school coaches do not confine their scouting activities to the National Championships. Many attend the district level meets and will sometimes identify for recruitment an athlete who did not perform well enough to make the district team; similarly coaches will recruit an athlete not selected for a parish team. This happens because the coach has spotted talent in the athlete who did not perform well on a given day. That approach is not new – Asafa Powell did not place in the first three in the 100 metres at CHAMPS and in fact up to the time he left secondary school, had not bettered 10.60 seconds in that

BEVERLEY McDONALD ▶

Graduated from an almost invincible high school sprinting career to win several sprint relay medals at the highest level, including gold at the 1991 Tokyo World Championships.

RISING STARS ✦✦

The CHAMPS line of production is unending; it ensures continuity in our athletics and this is evident in the accomplishments of these four young athletes, who, provided they transition fairly well to the senior level, will, along with others, carry on the great tradition of Jamaican athletics.

YOHAN BLAKE ▶

Bronze medallist in the 100m at the 2006 World Junior Championships and the fastest junior in that event in 2007 with a time of 10.11 seconds.

DEXTER LEE ▶

Gold medallist in the 100m at the 2007 World Youth Championships and also at the 2008 World Junior Championships.

RISING STARS ✦ ✦ ✦

▶ Did you know?

In 2007 Jamaica had the fastest 100 metres runners in the world in two age groups and the World Champion in a third: at the senior level, Asafa Powell, world record holder, 9.74 seconds; at the junior level (under 19 years), Yohan Blake, 10.11 seconds and at the youth level (under 18 years), Dexter Lee, gold medallist at the 2007 World Youth Championships.

RAMONE McKENZIE ▶

Gold medallist in the 200m at the 2007 World Youth Championships.

NICKEL ASHMEADE ▶

Silver medallist in the 100m and bronze medallist in the 200m at the 2007 World Youth Championships and silver medallist in the 200m at the 2008 World Junior Championships.

event. But he was identified by coach Stephen Francis as an athlete with talent to develop.

Although there is no special budgetary provision for coaches or physical education teachers at the primary, all age and junior high level, creative means are used to obtain the services of these personnel. In fact, most of the larger primary, all age and junior high schools have physical education teachers who would have been trained at the G.C. Foster College.

All the meets in the programme are funded by sponsorship of various types and supported by volunteers as there is no guaranteed Government support.

The value of the programme in the primary, all age and junior high schools, and in particular, the value of their National Championships, is very evident in the number of athletes from those Championships who have gone on to represent Jamaica at the Olympics and the World Championships. It is estimated that, over the past 20 years, more than 75 per cent of the athletes who have represented Jamaica performed at the National Championships. At the 2007 Osaka World Athletic Championships more than 90 per cent of the Jamaican team consisted of athletes who represented their parish at the National Championships. Outstanding products of those Championships are Veronica Campbell, many time medallist at the Olympics, 100 metres gold medallist at the 2007 Osaka World Championships, and recently 200 metres gold medallist at the Beijing Olympic Games; Usain Bolt, gold medallist and world record holder at the Beijing Olympic Games in the 100 metres, 200 metres and 4x100 metres relay; Sherone Simpson, world leader in the 100 and 200 metres in 2006 and silver medallist in the 100 metres at the Beijing Olympic Games; Trecia Smith, gold medallist in the triple jump at the 2005 World Championships; Shelly-Ann Fraser 100 metres gold medallist and Melaine Walker 400 metres hurdles gold medallist, both in Beijing. The Jamaica Teachers' Association and Blue Cross of Jamaica (the latter being long-standing sponsors of the National Championships) deserve the highest praise for the support they give to Jamaican athletics at this level.

In addition to the National Championships, the Institute of Sports has for the last 30 years organized an annual meet for the primary, all age and junior high schools in the Corporate Area, that is, the parishes of Kingston and St Andrew. The experience of this meet is that, organized as it is on the basis of schools rather than parishes, the competition is even keener than at the National Championships.

TRECIA-KAYE SMITH ▶

She broke new barriers winning the triple jump gold medal at the 2005 Helsinki World Championships – the first ever by a Jamaican in a field event at the global level.

AN HISTORIC PHOTOGRAPH – 100 YARDS FINAL – CHAMPS 1964

THEY'RE OFF: *(from left–right)* Clifton Forbes of Technical who came third; Michael Fray (St Andrew Technical); the winner, Lennox Miller of Kingston College (KC) who clocked 10.0 secs; Victor Lyle (Excelsior); Tony Keyes (KC); and second placed, Lewis Morris (Holmwood).

That CHAMPS is the training ground and launching pad for Jamaica's success at the international level is demonstrated by this photograph of the 100 yards final in 1964. Clifton Forbes, Michael Fray and Lennox MIller were members of the 4x100 metres relay team (the other member being Errol Stewart) that broke the world record at the 1968 Mexico Olympics in the heats and again in the semi-final, subsequently placing fourth in the final. Miller won a silver medal in the 100 metres at those Games and a bronze medal in the same distance at the 1972 Munich Olympic Games.

▶ Did you know?

Notwithstanding the spectacular advances made by our athletes, there is at least one national record that has stood for decades and represents a continuing challenge for our athletes and coaches.

Since the pioneering efforts of Arthur Wint in 1948 and 1952 in the 800 metres (silver medal at both Olympics), and Seymour Newman's national record of 1:45.21 seconds in 1977, Jamaica has not produced an athlete who has run below 1:45 seconds in that event.

Thus, the value of the athletic programme in the primary, all age and junior high schools in unearthing talent to be developed at the secondary level is well established.

The high calibre of athletes produced by the programme is indicated by Jamaica's outstanding performance at the regional level. Jamaica first entered the Caribbean Union of Teachers Biennial Track Meet – a regional meet for pre-secondary schools – in 2000, using that occasion to adjust to the novelty of the meet, and winning subsequently in 2004 and 2006.

Other Pre-Secondary Facilities

To complete the picture of track and field athletics in Jamaica up to the secondary level, it must be mentioned that there are facilities for basic school athletes (3–5 years). Additionally, there is the Preparatory Schools Championships (for private schools, children up to 11 years), which, like the national Primary, All Age and Junior High Schools Championships, is scouted by secondary school coaches for the recruitment of talented athletes. These meets are significant not so much for the athletes they produce as for the early exposure to organized athletics they provide for young Jamaicans. Importantly, they are also an indication of the extent to which running is a part of the culture of Jamaica.

5. *Features of the System*

SECONDARY LEVEL

THE FIRST FEATURE OF THE SYSTEM that accounts for the very high quality product in athletics is that today most secondary schools have a qualified coach; for that Jamaica must be grateful to the G.C. Foster College, where coaches are trained, and the JAAA, in particular, Teddy McCook who, in his long and productive tenure as that body's president, placed special emphasis on this aspect of athletic development in Jamaica. Teddy McCook is one of Jamaica's most experienced and distinguished sports administrators. Within the IAAF he is President of the North American, Central American and Caribbean Confederation (NACAC) as well as Jamaica's Council Area Representative. He has been awarded the Order of Jamaica, the country's fourth highest honour for his services to athletics.

No doubt Jamaica could have more qualified coaches, but to have as many as we do is a significant achievement.

JAMES BECKFORD ▶

His three silver medal performances at Olympic and World Championships, starting in Gothenburg, 1995, identify him clearly as Jamaica's best ever field event athlete.

Jamaica is fortunate to have had throughout its athletic history coaches such as G.C. Foster, Ted Lamont, Noel White, Herb McKenley, Foggy Burrowes, Carl March and Howard Jackson, who all had an understanding of the social significance of track and field athletics in promoting national pride. They, like all great coaches, did not merely impart technical knowledge; they were, in a larger sense, teachers and motivators, who helped to create and maintain the tradition of excellence in Jamaican athletics.

If one were to identify the single most important factor explaining Jamaica's sustained success in athletics, especially over the last two decades, it would have to be the extent and quality of the coaching available to athletes. Most of the coaches are graduates of the G.C. Foster College. The College, which was a gift of the Government of Cuba, was established in 1980. It has turned out thousands of graduates who work as coaches and physical education instructors in secondary and primary schools not only in Jamaica but also in other Caribbean countries. Prior to the establishment of the College, Jamaicans went abroad for training to become coaches and teachers in physical education. It was, until the Academy of Sports and Leisure was established in Trinidad and Tobago in 2007, the only Sports College in the English-speaking Caribbean. It trains specialist teachers in physical education and sports, offering a four year Bachelor of Physical Education Degree, a three year Diploma in Physical Education and a two year Certificate for coaches and accomplished sportsmen.

The G.C. Foster College and its graduates have had a transformational effect on Jamaican athletics.

Many of these coaches at times had to fund some of their young charges from their own pockets, as the basic needs of the sport – gear, special nutrition and transportation – were beyond the means of their parents. In such situations some coaches virtually assumed the role of parents.

Secondary schools are at the centre of the system that I am describing. The Annual Sports Day, where there is keen rivalry among school houses, is a microcosmic reflection and anticipation of the grander CHAMPS, where competition among schools is even keener. The system has benefited from the democratization of education over the past 50 years, which have seen the establishment of many new secondary schools. The pool from which athletes are drawn has therefore deepened. No longer is outstanding individual achievement at CHAMPS the preserve of students from what may be called the traditional ten or twelve schools. A record may be broken in an event by a boy or girl from a school of which little was known. This happens because that school has a

SHERONE SIMPSON ▶
See here securing her lane in the Beijing 200m final by placing 3rd in her semi-final round.

coach capable of nurturing a talent that may otherwise have gone unnoticed and underdeveloped. This is genuine progress and development.

There is greater motivation for athletes to work harder today than in the past. They have more support from their schools and their alumni; more attention is paid to their diet; some will have sponsorship for their track equipment, and importantly, there is the prospect of representing their country in many relatively new international meets, such as the World Youth Championships and the World Junior Championships at the global level, and regional meets such as Pan American Juniors, the Central American and Caribbean Juniors, and the CARIFTA Games, in which countries of the Caribbean Community and Common Market participate.

The second, and perhaps the most important feature of the system, is the rigour of the training regimen that prepares the athletes for CHAMPS. Here, the difference in eras is very marked. Forty to fifty years ago boys were little more than "gentlemen" athletes, who started training in January for CHAMPS in April. Today's athletes start training in September of the previous year for CHAMPS in March or April of the succeeding year. In some cases, they start from June or July, that is, a full nine or ten months before CHAMPS. An unfortunate consequence of this regimen is that some athletes do not participate in other sports such as cricket or football. The days of an all-rounder in the three major sports of athletics, cricket and football are, regrettably, gone.

One must also wonder what effect this regimen has on the academic work of the athletes, who may be in danger of becoming semi-professionalized.

An important feature of the training regimen – and again, this is vastly different from the period of 40 or 50 years ago – is that in almost every week from the middle of December to CHAMPS in March or April, there is at least one meet, usually on a Saturday, in which athletes test their mettle against each other. For example, on one particular Saturday, there is the Mannings Development Meet (Western Jamaica), the Morant Bay Relays (Eastern Jamaica), the North Central Development Meet (Central Jamaica) and the Big Shot Invitational (Kingston). Years ago there were two or three development meets prior to CHAMPS. In the present era in the JAAA's Calendar of Events there are usually listed about 27 preparatory and development meets prior to CHAMPS. Although there are so many meets in the relatively short period of four months, they are not treated casually by schools, coaches and athletes. They are taken very seriously. Interest and participation in these meets are exceptionally high; many of them take as long as 12 hours to be completed. It is nothing short of a phenomenon

KERRON STEWART ▶

Victorious in the 100m at the 2008 Jamaica National Championships, she went on to win silver in the 100m and bronze in the 200m at the Beijing Olympics.

that a school such as St Elizabeth Technical High School, in rural Jamaica, is able to attract athletes from over 60 schools for its Annual Invitational Meet; the more so, because it occurs on the same day and at the time that another meet – the Queens/Grace Jackson Invitational – is taking place in Kingston.

To achieve the quality product that school athletics in Jamaica represents, requires exceptional dedication and diligence. Nothing illustrates this more than these development meets which may call for a school at one end of the island to arrange for its athletes to travel on a Saturday to and from a parish at the other end, a distance of some 150 miles. Difficulties in transportation and shortage of funds are only overcome by dedication to the sport and the will to succeed.

Many bigger meets also precede CHAMPS and form an integral part of the training regimen for that massive athletic event. There are the Milo Western Relays, the Queens/Grace Jackson Invitational, the Gibson Relays, the University of the West Indies Track and Field Invitational, and the Eastern, Western, and Central Championships. In terms of training for a major athletic meet at the junior level, I doubt that any other country can match the depth and quality of the programme that prepares our athletes for CHAMPS.

The third factor is the institution itself, called CHAMPS. In 1910 there were six secondary schools and, perhaps, no more than 70 athletes competing at

CHAMPS. At CHAMPS in the present era some 85 boys' and 70 girls' schools and about 2,200 athletes (1,280 boys and 920 girls) participate. The Meet takes place at the National Stadium over a period of four days. It attracts the attention of every Jamaican, and there is scarcely another event in Jamaica that is as popular. CHAMPS is a rich and ever flourishing well-spring, producing high quality athletes year in, year out. Virtually, every Jamaican athlete who has excelled at the international level has run, jumped or thrown at CHAMPS. Here again, I very much doubt that any other country has an event that is CHAMPS' equal for quality in organization and performance, and for the excitement and intensity it generates.

Many foreign athletes, coaches and managers travel to Jamaica to study and benefit from our athletic system. Jacques Piasenta, a French coach, visited Jamaica. This is how his experience at CHAMPS was described in *L'Equipe* in an article entitled, "On Treasure Island: In quest of the secrets of Jamaican sprint . . .":[11]

Sport can be hypnotic. Twenty-five thousand people who rhythmically clap together to

SANDIE RICHARDS ▶
Her courage and character, running the 400m, shone like a beacon during 20 years of service at the junior and senior levels for Jamaica.

the same beat. Yeah man! Shouting and chanting the names of their favourite schools. Still clapping ten minutes after the end of a race. On a warm moonlit Saturday night in Kingston, this is the final act of the Boys and Girls High School Championships, Jamaica's most famous athletic meet. Three days earlier, Jacques Piasenta, a man with experience, had stated categorically that the Boys and Girls Championships had nothing over the UNSS Championships (Union Nationale du Sport Scolaire/National Organization for School Sport Activities) which he had been organizing for 3,000 youngsters from 1980 to 1987. But tonight, he is speechless: "I have been to seven consecutive Olympic Games, from Moscow straight through to Athens, and I have never experienced an atmosphere like this!"

Full credit must be given to ISSA, the JAAA, the schools, their coaches and supporters and the private sector for creating and sustaining what is indubitably one of the top athletic meets in the world for boys and girls under nineteen and a half years.

No praise can be too high for ISSA, which has been in existence for almost 100 years and has managed, with minimal resources, to produce this magnificent event that is CHAMPS. Make no mistake about it: it is participation at CHAMPS and the event itself that have inculcated in Jamaican athletes from a young age the willingness to put in the long hours required for training, the fire and the drive for competition, and the yearning for success – qualities that have prepared them for, and served them well at, the international level.

Jamaicans have a reputation for initiating major projects and enterprises. Regrettably, we are equally well-known for not maintaining them. Track and field athletics stands out as the exception. CHAMPS is the lubricant in the system that has sustained interest and performance in track and field athletics at the highest level for almost 100 years, and has kept it running smoothly and optimally for such a long period.

Evidence of the high quality of the product of the system at the junior level is provided by the following:

1. Several athletes have performed exceptionally well at the Olympics and World Championships while still at, or shortly after leaving school. Perhaps, the most outstanding are Una Morris (coached by Noel White), who at age 16 placed fourth in the 200 metres finals at the 1964 Tokyo Olympics; Raymond Stewart (coached by Glen Mills) who at the 1984 Los Angeles Olympics placed sixth in the finals of the 100 metres; Raymond Stewart and Gregory Meghoo, who were also members of the 4x100 metres relay

JULIET CUTHBERT ▶

Juliet had the good fortune to have been nurtured and trained at Morant Bay High School by one of Jamaica's greatest educators and coaches in athletics, the late Howard Jackson.

team that won the silver medal at the same Olympics; Veronica Campbell, who was a member of the team that won the silver medal in the 4x100 metres relay at the 2000 Sydney Olympics; Merlene Frazier, who was a member of the squad that won the gold medal in the 4x100 metres relay at the 1991 World Championships; Nikole Mitchell, who made the 100 metres final of the Stuttgart World Championships in 1993; and Aleen Bailey who was a member of the team that won the sprint relay bronze medal at the 1999 World Championships.

2. Jamaica has consistently performed well at the World Junior Championships and the World Youth Championships, with several athletes winning gold medals.

3. After 11 editions of the World Junior Championships, Gillian Russell remains, tied with Chris Nelloms of the USA, as the winner of the most gold medals – two in the 100 metres hurdles (1990 – Plovdiv; 1992 – Seoul) and two, leading off the 4x100 metres relay in the same Championships. In the total medal count, over the years Jamaicans, Nikole Mitchell (3x gold), Melaine Walker, and Russell, have won four – just behind the top medal winner, at five, East Germany's Katrin Krabbe.

4. Before breaking the world record in the 100 metres in 2008, Usain Bolt held the World Junior Record and the World Youth Record in the 200

metres. Bolt also has the distinction of being the youngest champion ever in the World Junior Championships, winning the 200 metres in Kingston in 2002 at the tender age of 15.

5. The records at CHAMPS are among the best performances in the world, particularly in the sprints, for that age group.

6. At the annual Penn Relays (in Pennsylvania, USA) Jamaican high schools regularly outperform their rivals from the USA. In fact, in the early days of our participation in those Relays, so outstanding were our schools, that it was thought by some in the USA that our athletes were members of All Star teams as distinct from school representatives.

7. At the CARIFTA Games Jamaica consistently outdistances the other countries.

USAIN BOLT ▶

World record holder in the 100 and 200m – 9.69 seconds and 19.30 seconds respectively – 2008 Beijing Olympic Games, August 16 and 20 respectively. His amazing and precocious talent was confirmed at age 15 by a World Junior Championships Gold Medal in the 200m in Kingston, Jamaica. A World Junior Record – 19.93 – was to follow in 2004.

$\mathcal{U}$SAIN "LIGHTNING" BOLT

Born: August 21, 1986

- **Holder of World Junior Record in All Age Groups**

  15 years, 20.58 seconds

  16 years, 20.13 seconds

  17 years, 19.93 seconds

  18 years, 19.93 seconds

  19 years, 19.88 seconds

- Youngest ever World Junior Champion at 15 years

- First junior to run 200 metres under 20 seconds

- Twice IAAF Rising Star of the Year

- Jamaican Class I (under 19 years) Boys' CHAMPS Record Holder in the 200 and 400 metres with times of 20.25 (2003) and 45.35 (2003) respectively

- Broke the Jamaican 200 metres record with a time of 19.75 seconds

- Silver medallist in the 200 metres at the 2007 Osaka World Athletic Championships

- World record holder 100 metres, 9.69 seconds, August 16, 2008 and the 200 metres, 19.30 seconds, August 20, 2008.

No Bolt out of the Blue!

A remarkable feature of the system is that it is not awash with financial resources. While there is some government and private sector support, generally, athletics in Jamaica is not well funded, and this serves to make the achievements all the more remarkable. Compared to football, which has not been as successful at the international level, athletics, in terms of funding, is very much the poor relative. It is strange that such a high quality product should suffer from a shortage of funds. Private sector companies in Jamaica should be "beating down the doors" of the JAAA, ISSA, schools, coaches, UTech and the G.C. Foster College to sponsor athletes and athletic events. There can be no doubt that they would receive value for their advertising dollar.

LORRAINE GRAHAM-FENTON ▶

She gave outstanding service, winning 400m sliver medals at the Olympic and World Championships levels, plus anchoring a 4x400m relay gold at the Edmonton Worlds in 2001.

6. *Features of the System*

PRIOR TO THE EARLY 1970S, THE DEVELOPMENT of Jamaican athletes proceeded in two stages, one local, and the other foreign. In the first stage the system described in the previous section took the athletes to the end of their secondary school career at age 18 or 19. Thereafter, our athletes went to colleges and universities in the USA for further development. Some of them succeeded. Names have already been mentioned, but it would not be unfair to say that a significant number never made it either on the track or in the classroom. The reasons are well known: difficulties in coping with a new environment, lack of financial resources – so-called scholarships never materialized – and being overworked on the track by their college coaches.

Nonetheless, Jamaica must be grateful to the USA for what it did in "finishing" our athletes. But note, without the foundation in Jamaica provided by the system to which I have referred, success in North American colleges or at the international level would not be attained.

It is ironic that the popularity of CHAMPS itself may have contributed to the vacuum in the training of adult athletes in Jamaica. The tendency was to see CHAMPS as the "be all and end all". The other factor explaining the void was that in that era there appears to have been a lack of interest on the part of tertiary educational institutions in the development of our athletes; the possibility of scholarships to the USA may also have led to complacency and tardiness in making provision for the training of our athletes at the adult level.

The College of Arts, Science and Technology (CAST), which was later to become the University of Technology (UTech), was the first institution to fill this void. An immense debt of gratitude is owed to UTech and CAST and in particular, to Dennis Johnson, who as the Director of Sports from 1971 to 2006, produced several athletes of international calibre, including Anthony Davis and Evan Clarke who made Olympic (Moscow 1980) and World Championships (Stuttgart 1993) teams, respectively. Dennis Johnson laid the basis for the present success of organized adult athletic training in Jamaica,

WINTHROP GRAHAM ▶

It took an amazing world record – 46.78 – to thwart his quest for 400m hurdles Olympic Gold in Barcelona 1992. Graham owed much of his success to the dedication of Mike Olivierre, his coach at St Elizabeth Technical High School (STETHS).

Glen Mills: The ahievements of his charge, triple gold medallist Usain Bolt in Beijing, confirmed his status as a coach of tremendous ability. He is one of the top two sprint coaches in the world.

and the achievements today of the Maximizing Velocity and Power (MVP) Club at UTech owe much to that foundation.

The G.C. Foster College also made its contribution to the training of adult athletes, and produced athletes, such as Devon Morris and Danny McFarlane, who represented Jamaica with distinction; both won silver medals at different Olympics, the former in 1988 and the latter in 2004.

Although in any sport success in coaching at the junior level is not necessarily a guarantee of success at the senior level, there have been over the years many capable and successful coaches at the secondary school level, whose record indicated that in all probability they would have had a smooth transition to coaching at the adult level. Foremost among these is Glen Mills, under whose guidance at Camperdown High School, Raymond Stewart became a first-class sprinter. Stewart at his first Olympics in 1984 at age 19 won all of his races in the heats and semi-final prior to the final of the 100 metres in which he placed sixth. This achievement was a clear indication of Glen Mills' ability to coach at the highest level. It should come as no surprise, therefore, that, in coaching at the High Performance Training Centre (HPTC) established by the IAAF in 2001 at UTech, he has had success with Usain Bolt, who won a silver medal in the 200 metres at the 2007 Osaka World Championships, and who in 2007 was ranked second in the world in that event. On May 3, 2008, Bolt ran the second fastest time ever in the 100 metres, 9.76 seconds, and on May 31, 2008 he broke the world record of his compatriot, Asafa Powell, with a time of 9.72 seconds. He is now the world record holder in both the 100 and 200 metres. Glen Mills, who has been awarded the Order of Distinction by the Government of Jamaica, deserves greater national recognition for the success he has had in coaching over such a long period.

Outstanding secondary school coaches include: Michael Clarke of Calabar High School, who has the distinction of being the only person in the modern era to have coached three secondary schools (St Jago High School, Jamaica College and Calabar High School) to victory at CHAMPS;[12] Raymond "K.C." Graham, formerly of St Jago High School; Lennox Graham, formerly of Kingston College; and Maurice Wilson, formerly of Holmwood Technical High School, now the coach at the G.C. Foster College.

When a product, such as Jamaica's Secondary-Junior Athletic Programme, is the best in the world, it is bound to attract worldwide attention. Who are the coaches to have produced this high quality product? Not surprisingly, in the USA, colleges have

ALEEN BAILEY ▶

Gained selection on two World Championships teams (Athens, 1997; Seville, 1999) while still in high school, executed a spirited third leg and safe handoff to ensure the gold medal for Jamaica at the 2004 Athens Olympics.

Maurice Wilson: Has made the smooth and compelling transition from a top performing high school coach to place three athletes, all quarter milers, on the Beijing team, two gaining relay medals.

shown interest in tapping into this deep reservoir of coaching talent, and both Raymond Graham and Lennox Graham have gone to work in the USA. They are not the first and no doubt will not be the last. This reflects very favourably on the quality of the Junior Programme. But, one must hope that our coaches do not become major contributors to the braindrain that has had such a negative impact on Jamaica's growth and development.

Stephen Francis is the best example of a coach who has moved successfully from the junior to the senior level. He has been awarded the Order of Distinction by the Government of Jamaica, and his work must be highlighted because of its significance for the development of adult athletic training in Jamaica.

Stephen Francis first trained athletes at his alma mater, Wolmer's High School for Boys, where he made a name for himself as an accomplished coach. In 1999 along with his brother Paul, David Noel, and Bruce James, he established the MVP Track and Field Club. Some of the athletes in the Club have been recruited to enter UTech. His charges include Asafa Powell, the former holder of the 100 metres World Record, and Sherone Simpson, the 2006 world ranked number 1 in both the 100 and 200 metres and silver medallist in the 100 metres at the Beijing Olympic Games. It is an outstanding achievement for a coach to have trained in a given year not only the world record holder in an athletic event for men, but also the world leader in two events for women. This achievement of Stephen Francis and the MVP Club, which may very well be without precedent, must fill every Jamaican with a great sense of pride. He is also the coach of Shelly-Ann Fraser, gold medallist in the 100 metres, Melaine Walker, gold medallist in the 400 metres hurdles and Germaine Mason who won a silver medal for the UK in the high jump, at the Beijing Olympic Games.

Whereas formerly, adult athletic training in Jamaica was, apart from that which was done at CAST and UTech, occasional, episodic, confined to a small group of individuals and only relatively successful, Stephen Francis has established a standing and well-organized body that now has upwards of 50 athletes, and has been so successful that he is attracting athletes from other countries, for example, Darrell Brown of Trinidad and Tobago, the 2003 World Championships 100 metres silver medallist, and South African sprinter, Geraldine Pillay. With the former 100 metres world record holder and others of the quality of Sherone Simpson in his camp, the day may not be far off when any indebtedness to the USA for "finishing" our athletes will be repaid by Stephen Francis and other Jamaican coaches "finishing" athletes from the USA in Jamaica.

DELLOREEN ENNIS LONDON ▶

Back from career-threatening injury in 2001, when Edmonton World Championships glory seemed likely, her outstanding achievements – Helsinki World Championships silver in 2005, Osaka World Championships bronze in 2007 and Pan Am Games gold, Rio de Janeiro, 2007 – spoke volumes of her resilience.

Stephen Francis: The impressive impact of his singular contribution to the Beijing Olympics was rooted in the magnificent performance of his charges. Had his athletes been able to compete as a country in the Olympics, his MVP Club would have placed sixth in the medal tables. Stephen is one of the top two sprint coaches in the world.

Stephen Francis, the MVP Club, the HPTC and UTech are to be congratulated for successfully establishing in Jamaica a parallel to the North American system of combining university education with athletic development – something that should have been done long ago by our premier tertiary educational institution, the University of the West Indies. Of course, the example of scholarship and athletic talent had been set long ago by Norman Manley. In that regard, gratitude must also be expressed to Olympic Solidarity, the outreach arm of the IOC, for the scholarships and financial assistance it has given to Sherone Simpson, Usain Bolt and Germaine Gonzales. Also to be thanked are those private sector companies that have provided similar assistance to our athletes.

The work of the MVP Club, the HPTC and UTech merely provides confirmation of the immense talent of our secondary school coaches. If there was ever any doubt about the quality and potential of those coaches, it has been dispelled by the achievements of Glen Mills, the HPTC, Stephen Francis and the MVP Club. Glen Mills and Stephen Francis are among the best sprint coaches in the world.

There are some international commentators who have a tendency to describe a Jamaican athlete exclusively in terms of the American college that he or she attended. There is no acknowledgement of the system in Jamaica that provided the athletes with the foundation to succeed at the adult level. With the continuing development of the adult athletic programme, as evidenced by the achievements of Glen Mills, the HPTC, Stephen Francis and the MVP Club, the basis for that practice, which detracts from the Jamaicanness of the performance of our athletes at the international level, will disappear. For Usain, Asafa, Shelly-Ann, Sherone and Shericka born ya, grow ya and train ya.[13]

One does not wish to appear unduly defensive or sensitive about the contribution that colleges in the USA have made to Jamaican athletics, but that contribution must be placed in context. A comparison may be made with the contribution that county cricket in the United Kingdom made to West Indies cricket. There was a time when many of the top West Indian cricketers played county cricket in England, and undoubtedly their game and the standard of our cricket benefitted from that exposure; that was particularly the case when the West Indians dominated world cricket for a period of 20 years. Michael Manley's (former Prime Minister of Jamaica) assessment of the contribution of county cricket to West Indies cricket cannot be faulted. He wrote, "Clearly county cricket made a major contribution to the

DANNY McFARLANE ▶

The essence of determination and grit – not even a late career change to the 400m hurdles could prevent him from wining a silver medal at the 2004 Athens Olympic Games, where his basic 400m speed was definitely an asset.

evolution of our Test sides. It toughened the core of the team, but it certainly did not create the team or make the team great.[14]" By the same token, USA colleges did not make Jamaican athletics great; that distinction belongs to the first-class programme that has existed in our secondary schools for decades.

It is ironic that the negative view that some foreigners had of Jamaica's adult athletic programme may well be the explanation for its present success. At a sprint workshop in Trinidad and Tobago, Paul Francis, brother of Stephen, read a paper prepared by Stephen. In that paper Stephen wrote that in 1998 at the World Junior Championships in France, he listened as coaches from the USA said: "Coaching teenagers is nothing, just baby-sitting. They are growing so fast that it does not require astute coaching skills to get them to improve. When they stop growing is when the real coaching comes into play at 19 for girls, age 20 to 21 for men. You people in Jamaica can't coach. All you do is keep the teenagers ready and interested until we, the real coaches, take over."[15]

The assessment that coaching teenagers does not require any skill is invalid, and must be seen as a not so subtle attempt to devalue the achievements of what is the best junior athletic programme in the world. Nonetheless, stung by this harsh criticsm, Stephen Francis then and there decided to establish the MVP Track Club. And how have Glen Mills and Stephen Francis, coaches of the two fastest runners in history, wholly trained in Jamaica, made those coaches from the USA eat their words!

In light of Stephen Francis' distinguished pedigree in coaching, his success is not surprising. He was influenced by Dennis Johnson in the latter's time at CAST, and Dennis himself, a former holder of the 100 yards World Record, was coached by the great Bud Winter of the USA. Bud Winter guided his athletes, including Tommie Smith and Lee Evans, to 37 world records.

That the success of Stephen Francis and the MVP Club with Asafa Powell, Sherone Simpson, Michael Frater, Brigitte Foster-Hylton and others is not a "flash in the pan", is demonstrated by the performance of Kaliese Spencer at the 2006 World Junior Championships in Beijing. Here is an athlete who placed sixth in the 800 metres at CHAMPS in 2005, following which she commenced training for the 400 metres hurdles in September with the MVP Club. In the short time of ten months she ran 55.11 seconds for the gold medal in Beijing. Considering that the 400 metres hurdles is viewed by many as the most difficult event in track, and that many adult athletes spend years trying to break 55 seconds, this is a remarkable achievement.

MAURICE SMITH ▶

An outstanding performer on the big day. All Jamaica hailed his historic and unexpected silver medal in the decathlon at the 2007 Osaka World Championships and hope that his achievement will encourage other Jamaicans to take up this event.

The social and economic significance of what Stephen Francis and the MVP Club are doing at UTech appears to have escaped most Jamaicans. It is not to indulge in hyperbolic comment to say that they are doing for athletics in Jamaica what Marcus Garvey, Norman Manley and Alexander Bustamante did for our political life years ago. For what they are doing, and doing successfully, is nothing less than liberating Jamaica's athletes from dependency on a foreign system. They are in the company of a number of other Jamaicans – for example, Louise Bennett in speech, Rex Nettleford in dance, and Bob Marley in music – whose efforts have succeeded in promoting the development of something that is uniquely Jamaican, and more important, have contributed to the development of a national identity. None of this is to say that foreign influence or foreign aid is bad. Indeed, as Professor Trevor Munroe stressed, the modern era of globalization calls for "the most thorough mastery of the best that the global environment has to offer" in all areas of national endeavour.[16] However, what is bad and altogether negative is a syndrome of dependency on foreign influence or aid that stifles the growth of self reliance and independence.

I place Stephen Francis, the other founders of the MVP Club and Glen Mills in that band of Jamaicans who, through their efforts, have demonstrated that we can attain standards as high as those in any other country, and that whatever the field of endeavour is, be it athletics, law, medicine, education or agriculture, we do not need to be coached or validated by outsiders in order to succeed. Self-doubt is the worst relic of our past and in some important areas of national life remains an unyielding blight on growth and development.

Training at the post-secondary level is also done at the IAAF's HPTC at UTech, of which Teddy McCook is the administrator, and at which Fitz Coleman is the coach. The G.C. Foster College also provides training at the adult level. Maurice Wilson, one of the most successful coaches at the junior level, is now the coach at that college, which has among its students some of the talented athletes he trained at Holmwood Technical High School.

There are other facilities for adult athletic training on a smaller scale. No doubt some of these have been inspired by the success of the MVP Club. Some of the more successful coaches at the secondary level have instituted senior training programmes, attracting some of their former charges as well as others.

In the MVP Club, the HPTC and the G.C. Foster College, Jamaica has three high

NOVELENE WILLIAMS ▶

Her steady improvement over the years took her to the final of the 400m at Osaka, where, but for a slightly misjudged race, she might have come away with the gold medal.

quality institutions for adult athletes, which have demonstrated that they are more than an adequate replacement of, or alternative to the training facilities in the USA. They now function as an integral part of the system I have described, complementing, at the adult level, the well-tried system at the junior level. Adult athletic training, which for many years lagged behind the junior programme, is now matching strides with that programme.

In the third edition of *Jamaican Athletics: A Model for the World*, a preview of Jamaica's prospects for the Beijing Olympics was offered. It has been retained at Annex III for the purposes of comparative analysis. The medals won in Beijing as well as the Finalists are also set out in that Annex.

7. *Areas For Stronger Focus*

NOTWITHSTANDING JAMAICA'S WELL-DESERVED reputation in global track and field athletics, it has to be conceded that – and this is confirmed by an examination of the records in Annexes IV to IX – this reputation has been earned almost exclusively on the basis of its athletes excelling in a select set of events – the sprints, the relays, long jump and triple jump. We should not be content with that. We must redouble our efforts to improve in the longer track events, as well as the throwing events. It is in fact embarrassing that, following upon the pioneering efforts of Arthur Wint in 1948 and 1952 in the 800 metres (silver medal at both Olympics), and Seymour Newman's national record of 1:45.21 seconds in 1977, we have not produced an athlete who has run below 1:45 seconds in that event.

An encouraging aspect in the development of adult athletics is the recent improvement of the following athletes who have achieved international standards in events that may be considered non-traditional for Jamaica: Maurice Smith and Claston Bernard in the decathlon – Smith performed beyond expectations, winning the silver medal at the 2007 Osaka World Championships – Dorian Scott in the shot put and Olivia McKoy in the javelin.

There is absolutely no reason why, with adequate coaching, Jamaicans should not excel in these events. What is missing is the interest of young athletes. To generate this interest, special incentives should be offered at the junior and senior level to athletes who excel in discus, shot put, javelin and the decathlon; incentives should also be given to their coaches.

Maurice Smith's outstanding achievement at the World Championships is bound to motivate Jamaican athletes to devote more time to the decathlon. It is the throwing events and the pole vault on which more emphasis needs to be placed if we are to improve in the multidisciplinary events.

Significantly, Dorian Scott, who consistently throws over 20 metres, reached the final of the shot put at both the 2007 World Championships and the 2008 World Indoor Championships. Scott's heave of 21.45 metres on March 28, 2008, which broke his own Jamaican record, was at that time the longest throw in the world for 2008. Scott's achievement will undoubtedly inspire young Jamaicans to concentrate on the shot put. The hope must be that the influence of Maurice Smith, Dorian Scott and others will transform the decathlon and the weight events from non-traditional to traditional events in Jamaica.

An oddity in our track and field programme is the absence of the javelin from the Boys' Championships, even though it features in the Girls'. ISSA and the sponsors should act immediately to introduce this event in the Boys' Championships so as to ensure that our male athletes do not experience that event for the first time as seniors.

In Germaine Mason, Jamaica has a high jumper of international standard. Mason, who now holds the Jamaican record of 2.34 metres, was a member of Stephen Francis' MVP Club. However, he decided to represent the country of his birth, the United Kingdom, and went there to live. Interestingly, he returned to Jamaica to train with his former coach at the MVP Club, while still retaining his UK team position. It is gratifying to note this reaffirmation of his faith in the quality of the coaching staff of the MVP Club. His confidence in Stephen Francis was confirmed by his silver medal for the UK at the Beijing Olympics. We must ensure that coaching and training are at a level to produce more male high jumpers of international standard.

Considering that Diane Guthrie's national record of 1.90 metres in the high jump was set in 1992, and that the qualifying mark for the World Championships is 1.95

SHERICKA WILLIAMS ▶
One of the locally-based athletes in the MVP Club, she produced an astonishing late run in the 400m to take silver at the Beijing Olympics.

metres, we should now be working to produce our first female athlete to reach, or better that standard.

To the areas of concern must, regrettably, be added the 400 metres for men. Jamaica had no finalist in the flat event in Beijing and came last in the 4x400 metres relay. Indeed, Ricardo Chambers is the only Jamaican capable of running fairly consistently below 45 seconds. Again, legacy and history should provide the motivation. It is in the 400 metres flat and the relay that Jamaica made its name at the international level in 1948 and 1952 through the individual and collective exploits of Wint, Rhoden, McKenley and Laing. The men must pull up their socks. The 400 metres, after all, is a sprint. The men must draw level with the women, three of whom have run below 50 seconds (which is generally taken as the gender equivalent to a male sub-45 seconds). However, in a country where men are accustomed to being outperformed by women, Jamaican men might have had some satisfaction watching the Jamaican male sprint quartet showing their female counterparts how to pass the baton around fairly conservatively and still break the world record.

8. Why is Jamaican Athletics a Model for the World?

THE FEATURES CONSTITUTING THE JAMAICAN ATHLETIC environment, in particular the junior programme, may be emulated by any country, developed or developing. But it would be of particular value to the poorer developing countries, since it shows how a country can attain the highest global standards with relatively little funding.

Practically all the components in the Jamaican athletic environment are replicable by other countries. What may not be readily replicable is the Jamaican passion for athletics that is partially the result of the country's rich legacy in a sport that has produced a multitude of heroes and heroines and with it a culture of adoration for them. But the passion is also the result of the way in which the athletic programmes, particularly at the secondary–junior level, are organized. That feature can certainly be emulated.

The main lesson to be learnt from Jamaican athletics is the importance of having trained coaches: talent needs to be instructed, nurtured and guided. For that purpose, a

79

▶ Did you know?

Of the 14 parishes in Jamaica, Trelawny has the highest number of Jamaican representatives and world class athletes: Anecdotally, the explanation for the pre-eminence of Trelawny in Jamaican athletics is nutrition based: the high quality of the yams in that parish.

Women
  Veronica Campbell-Brown
  Debbie-Ann Paris
  Audrey Reid
  Dorothy Scott
  Inez Turner
  Janice Turner
  Yvette Turner
  Astia Walker
  Rosemarie Whyte

Men
  Marvin Anderson
  Usain Bolt
  Omar Brown
  Ricardo Chambers
  Lindel Frater
  Michael Frater
  Michael Green
  Ben Johnson
  George Kerr

country needs to have access to an educational institution, such as the G.C. Foster College, to equip persons with the skills to coach and train athletics.

Another component of Jamaican athletics that is worthy of emulation is the relationship between athletics and educational institutions, whether at the primary, secondary or tertiary level; they provide a natural accommodation for the development of skills in all sports, including athletics. But some countries do not appreciate the value of this linkage, leaving children at the secondary level to develop their skills in clubs rather than at schools.

The emphasis placed by the Jamaican athletic system on intra- and inter-schools rivalry is equally significant. Rivalry within a school between different houses serves to promote interest in the sport, and of course, there is no substitute for rivalry between schools. Here the component that warrants special attention is the organization of a grand event, such as CHAMPS, to generate interest and sharpen competition. But that calls for a body such as ISSA that is devoted to the organization of athletics among secondary schools.

A key feature of the Jamaican athletic system to which other countries should pay particular attention is the intensity of the training regimen. Other countries may wish to institute development meets along the lines of those taking place on a Saturday in Jamaica over a three-month period in preparation for a big event such as CHAMPS.

But countries must not concentrate on athletes at the secondary-junior level to the detriment of the development of an efficient programme at the senior level. This was a mistake made by Jamaica for a very long time. Tertiary educational institutions should be encouraged to attract top class athletes from the secondary schools into a programme with an appropriate stress on scholarship and athletic development. While clubs may not be suitable for the development of athletes at the secondary level, they certainly are at the senior level. Coaches who succeed at the secondary level may also succeed at the tertiary level, and they should consider establishing clubs, such as Stephen Francis' MVP Club, which has among its members Asafa Powell, Sherone Simpson, Shelly-Ann Fraser and Melaine Walker. Moreover, clubs may have a working relationship with a tertiary educational institution, such as the MVP Club has with the University of Technology.

The development of a successful senior programme is critically important for poorer countries, whose athletes may not have the resources to go abroad for training. The Jamaican experience suggests that it may not take a long time to develop a successful senior programme.

Jamaicans must not be lulled into complacency by our success. All Jamaicans have a duty to do everything in their power to ensure that the environment that has yielded

> **Did you know?**

At the 1952 Helsinki Olympic Games, Herb McKenley ran the third leg of the 4x400 metres relay in the fantastic time of 44.6 seconds. Many calculations have been made over the years to compare McKenley's time to the performance of today's athletes; all of these calculations have the same result: they show that his time of 44.6 seconds on a cinder track, in contrast to the modern and faster synthetic surface, must rank as one of the greatest 400 metres ever run in any era.

this world class product in track and field athletics is preserved. Specific cultural progammes should be developed, particularly in schools, to highlight the country's rich legacy in global athletics. The structural and systemic features that have served us so well are in need of, and should receive greater financial support from the Government, the private sector, and indeed from all Jamaicans.

In light of the heights of excellence attained by track and field athletics, the fame and glory that it has brought to Jamaica and the important role of schools in the athletic system, no school should ever want for athletic equipment and gear. It is scandalous that not more than ten secondary schools possess a full set of hurdles, an event in which the basic requirement – speed – is not in short supply in Jamaica. The country must wake up to its responsibility to this unique product.

At the same time, countries seeking to develop or improve their athletic programme can look at the Jamaican experience, and adopt those components that are suitable for their environment and culture.

9. *Transferring Best Practices in Track and Field Athletics to the Wider Society*

THE QUESTIONS POSED EARLIER DESERVE SOME COMMENT: if with such limited resources, Jamaica can excel in one area of national life, why can't we do the same in others? Can the practices in track and field be used to our advantage in other areas of national life?

Professor Trevor Munroe, in his incisive analysis of *Jamaican Athletics: A Model for the World*, devoted some time to these burning and difficult issues. Professor Munroe extracted five features of the track and field athletic system, as outlined in the book, and which, in his view, could be usefully translated to the wider society: developing local practices by fuller exposure to global best practice; healthy competition but with less tribalism; more coaching, upskilling, more knowledge of role models and historic figures; greater autonomy within a common policy framework for key players in the system of governance; and new qualities of volunteerism at all levels in the system of governance.[17]

The questions are relevant, because if the best practices from track and field athletics are replicated in other areas of national life, it is very likely that the success in athletics would not be the isolated oasis of excellence it appears to be.

By far the most important element of the Jamaican athletic environment that warrants emulation in the wider society is the unifiying spirit and the community of interest that characterize the relationship between the principal actors. If the divisiveness and tribalism that are features of political life and governance in Jamaica were replaced by the sense of community and solidarity present in track and field athletics, there can be little doubt that there would be higher levels of performance and output. This is not to say that the athletic environment is without blemish. But one does not hear a Jamaican ask whether Usain Bolt, Asafa Powell or Veronica Campbell-Brown is a supporter of the Jamaica Labour Party (JLP) or the Peoples National Party (PNP) – the two rival political parties that have governed Jamaica since adult suffrage in 1944. Nor has anyone ever asked whether Herb McKenley was a supporter of the JLP or PNP – an unconcern rendered the more telling by the fact that he was once a candidate in parliamentary elections. For the environment in which track and field athletics operates has served to render such questions irrelevant, with the result that the lens through which an athlete and his achievements are viewed is not smudged by the bias of political partisanship. An athlete is, first and last, a Jamaican.

Another lesson which the wider Jamaican society can learn from track and field athletics is that if international standards are to be attained, systems must be put in place to ensure the production of the highest quality trained personnel. There is an obvious advantage when there are local institutions, such as the G.C. Foster College, to train trainers. But if there isn't any, or if what there is, is not adequate, then we must seek the best that the global market has to offer. Although the majority of Jamaica's track and field coaches and trainers are graduates of the G.C. Foster College, not all of them are: some are trained abroad. The knowledge base of trained personnel must be as deep and as wide as possible, drawing from all sources, local and foreign.

It is difficult to overstress the significance of the achievement of Stephen Francis and Glen Mills. They have demonstrated that home-grown athletes can be as good as, if not better than, USA-based athletes. The coaches in Jamaica are brilliant. They have as much expertise as those from the USA; arguably, in many cases, they are more highly skilled. The lesson for a people who have been socialized through centuries of foreign domination into thinking that the foreign is always better than the local is that, no matter what the discipline, Jamaicans can attain the same heights of excellence as any foreigner. By their example of self-confidence,

SHELLY-ANN FRASER ▶
Beijing 100m queen, cool and unperturbed, cruising to a 100m second round win in Beijing.

self-reliance, dedication to task and the application of the highest professional standards, Stephen Francis and Glen Mills have demonstrated that Jamaicans can, to echo the rallying cry of Marcus Garvey, *accomplish what they will*.[19]

But those heights of excellence are not attained easily. They are only achieved on the basis of application and hard work. Athletics teaches the importance of discipline, commitment and perseverance.

The comments of Germaine Mason, the Jamaican high jumper, who won a silver medal for the UK, and who trained with Stephen Francis in Jamaica, are instructive. Describing Stephen Francis as being like a strict father to his children, he said, "We get up at five in the morning, which a lot of athletes think is ridiculous, but it is part of being disciplined and wanting to achieve whatever goal you want. You cannot party, you cannot drink. It is difficult, but it works."[20]

When, as has been proposed,[21] Jamaica capitalizes on its athletic assets by the creation of an industry providing worldwide services in athletics, the sport will have taught another important lesson: Jamaica does not have to remain a net importer and consumer of know-how; it can and must become a net exporter and producer of many types of intellectual property.

The achievements of Shelly-Ann Fraser and Melaine Walker, gold medallists in Beijing and who are both from troubled inner-city communities[22] illustrate that an individual with talent need not be limited by his or her own circumstances, but can, with discipline and determination, rise above those circumstances to become the best in the world. This resolve was well expressed by Shelly-Ann's mother, who after watching her daughter win Olympic gold, said "This is to show that something good can come out of the ghetto. Ghetto can't hold you back as long as you have ambition".[23] Shelly-Ann's emphatic victory punch in the 100 metres must then be seen for what it is – a symbol of her triumph over the challenges she has faced.

Athletics also teaches the value of patience, which is required in so many areas, for example, the transition from junior to the senior level, waiting for months or a year for recovery from an injury and waiting for the recovery of form that has been lost.

Claims for the exemplary role of athletics in national life should not be exaggerated. But when an enterprise has been as consistently successful as Jamaican athletics in developing and sustaining a product of the highest international standard, there must be something of value to be extracted from its practices for the benefit of the wider society.

MELAINE WALKER ▶
Melaine Walker, another St Jago High School product, hunting gold and Olympic record status in Beijing.

10. *The 2008 Beijing Olympic Games*

EVERY COUNTRY HAS ITS HISTORIC, epochal moments that are etched in the collective consciousness of its people. More often than not these are events that capture the imagination, stir national pride, and provide platforms from which the nation can lift itself to a higher plane. Some of those events are catastrophes evoking both national mourning and regret. Jamaica has experienced such periods in the aftermath of the crushing of Sam Sharpe's Christmas Rebellion in 1831, in the savagery of the repression which followed the Morant Bay Rebellion in 1865 and in the deaths of the strikers killed in the 1938 Labour Rebellion.

However, others are occasions of national triumph which evoke national celebration and which refresh, restore or regenerate the people's faith in the limitlessness of the national potential to achieve by hard and purposeful work. For some reason these happy periods often occur for Jamaica in the summer months.

On August 1, 174 years ago we thronged the streets and filled the churches in celebration of Emancipation, the beginning of the end of a dreadful period in our country's history and the beginning of our continuing transition towards a society in which Jamaicans are truly free and equal under the law.

On August 6, 46 years ago, we were again in the streets and the churches and this time we also filled our new National Stadium in celebration of Jamaica's Independence, the beginning of our still-continuing emergence into national maturity as a State, sovereign not only in law but in resolve and deed.

These two celebrations were outpourings of joy at political events of unquestionable significance. But the summer months have also seen us celebrating other events whose importance may seem questionable in the minds of some.

I refer first to the Second Test Match in the West Indies tour of England in 1950 when Jamaica joined with the West Indies in jubilation at the achievements of a great team, proclaiming once and for all that there was no prize in cricket beyond the reach of the Caribbean people. The colonized had vanquished the colonizer.

There was the celebration for Jamaica's victory over the USA at the 1952 Helsinki Olympic Games in the 4x400 metres relay – an achievement the significance of which was aptly reflected in the headlines in Jamaica's *Daily Gleaner:* "Jamaica Beats the World".

▶ Did you know?

When Jamaica won the men's and women's 100 and 200 metres at the Beijing Olympic Games, it was the first time since the 1988 Seoul Olympic Games that a country achieved that feat.

He occupies "A DIFFERENT WORLD" in "A DIFFERENT RACE". Usain Bolt scoffs at the challenge from the Rest of the World with a Beijing 100m win in record breaking distance margin in the electronic timing era, 9.69:9.89, equalling Carl Lewis (USA); Sam Graddy (USA) 9.99:10.19, Los Angeles, 1984.

Then there was also that marvellous period in 1998 when all of Jamaica celebrated the historic participation of the Reggae Boyz in Football's World Cup Finals in France.

But, apart from Emancipation Day and Independence Day, which are obviously the most memorable days in Jamaica, no event or moment has stirred national pride and given rise to as much joy and celebration as the glorious nine days in August 2008 when Jamaica dazzled the rest of the world with its amazing feats in Beijing.

From a field of 204 countries Jamaica placed third in track and field athletics at those Games, with only the USA and Russia in front. The six gold, three silver and two bronze medals won by our athletes represent Jamaica's best medal haul at the Olympics and rank as its best performance in global athletics. Thus, Jamaica with a population of 2.8 million and a per capita income of US$4,600 placed ahead of many larger and much better-resourced countries, such as Germany, France, Canada and

BOLT WITH SHOES IN OUTSTRETCHED ARMS

Usain Bolt, after one of his gold medal world record breaking runs, does a well-timed marketing job for his Puma brand.

the Scandinavian countries. The UK, with whom Jamaica shares historical links, did not achieve its own very modest target of five medals in track and field athletics.[24] Though Jamaica was third in track and field athletics at the 1948 London and the 1952 Helsinki Games, this performance must be more highly regarded because of the number and quality of medals won and the number of participating countries. The depth in the quality of the team is evident in the number of athletes who, apart from the medallists, reached the final of many events. A list of the medallists as well as the non-medallists who reached the final in their events is set out in Annex III.

A rare experience for Jamaica – and a lesson for the wider society – was that the expectation and promise of one day was matched by fulfilment in the next. Victory and success came in such proportions that, when the Jamaican women failed to pass the baton around in the 4x100 metres relay, it was remarked by a Jamaican lady that God was punishing us for the sins of avarice and hubris. In the same vein, when Jamaica placed last in the 4x400 metres men's relay, Michael Johnson, former world record holder in the 200 metres and BBC commentator, was heard to say, "At last Jamaica has come last in a race." The performance of the Jamaican athletes attracted the attention of the entire world, with journalists and foreigners asking how a small country could do so well in the Olympics. Of course, it was not the first time that that question was being asked.

Jamaica's domination of the short sprints was astounding and impressive: victory in the 100, 200 and 4x100 metres (men) in world record time; victory in the 100 metres (women), winning all three medals; and gold and bronze in the 200 metres (women). The Beijing Olympic Games confirmed Jamaica's status as the sprint capital of the world.

The Beijing exploits of the athletes brought joy and pride to every Jamaican. The mood of a country, racked by division and in the grip of spiralling crime and economic hardship, was transformed by the achievements of the athletes. Morale was lifted. There

▶ Did you know?

Usain Bolt's victory in the 100 metres and Veronica Campbell-Brown's victory in the 200 metres were achieved by, roughly, the same margin – 2/10ths of a second.

Usain Bolt's victory in the 100 and 200 metres was the first in those events since 1988 at the Olympic Games.

The triumphant triumvirate shows Jamaica's dominance in the sprints – Golden Girl, the "Pocket Rocket" Shelly-Ann Fraser (lane 3) with an unmistakable victory punch; Sherone Simpson (lane 2) and Kerron Stewart (lane 6) an unprecedented silver and silver.

was celebration in every nook and cranny of Jamaica. All Jamaicans, young, old, rich and poor, the public and private sector, supporters of the two rival political parties, were overjoyed. Patriotic fervour was at a peak, and the Jamaican flag was everywhere to be seen. The achievements of the athletes had succeeded, where all else had failed, in unifying the country, if only for a short period. Jamaicans abroad also followed the Olympics very closely and had their own celebrations. The Jamaican Government, sensitive to the lessons for the wider society from the Beijing Olympics, organized celebrations islandwide over a period of four days, and announced plans to establish a Centre of International Sporting Excellence.

In Usain Bolt Jamaica had the most spectacular performer of the Beijing Games. The winner of three gold medals – all in world record time – Usain, the athlete and the showman, thrilled the crowd and was easily the most popular athlete of the Games. Amazingly, he virtually stopped running after about 85 of the 100 metres, and yet still broke the world record. He also had time to slap his chest in triumph and, following the race, broke into dance showing the latest Jamaican Dance Hall moves – the "Gully Creepa" and "Nuh Linga" – to the world. These innocuous antics incurred the wrath of IOC President, Count Jacques Rogge, who criticized Usain for not showing more respect to his fellow athletes. Count Rogge's insensitivity to the playful exhibition of the cultural practices of one of the 204 countries participating in the Olympics was not shared by others. On August 21 Usain was regaled in song by the massive crowd in Beijing's Bird Nest Stadium chanting "Happy Birthday". In fact, Usain's personality was so mesmeric and he so endeared himself to the Olympic community that his name appears to have slipped into the language: when a television commentator observed that a runner had slackened his pace considerably some distance from the finish line, he described the victory as "Boltesque". Usain brought a dimension to the Beijing Olympics that made it the spectacle it might not otherwise have been.

But the most outstanding performance of the Games was

◄ Shelly-Ann Fraser celebrates her 100m victory.

The awesome threesome. Olympic 100m gold medallist Shelly-Ann Fraser *(centre)* and silver medallists Kerron Stewart *(left)* and Sherome Simpson *(right)* show off their medals following a Jamaican clean sweep of the women's 100m final.

Veronica Campbell-Brown's win in the 200 metres. Her performance is more highly rated than Usain's because, although both won by the same margin, in Alyson Felix she faced stiffer competition than Usain did in either of his two individual events. She recognized that she could only prevail if she had a match-winning strategy and executed it to perfection. Veronica knew that the only way she could win was to use her superior 100 metres speed to get to the bend first, run it hard, and come off with a defensible lead over Felix; thereafter, it was catch me if you can. The fear that Felix's much vaunted 400 metres

World Champion Veronica Campbell-Brown (2133), an emphatic
Beijing 200m gold (21.74), wresting the initiative from the struggling
USA's 2007 200m World Champion Alyson Felix (3167), with Jamaica's
Kerron Stewart (2178) securing the bronze .

strength would power her past Veronica in the last 40 metres was never realized. In winning the gold medal, Veronica succesfully defended her title and bettered her personal record by 2/10ths of a second. Veronica's experience shows that at the highest level natural talent must be supported by mental toughness and determination.

Jamaica completed a clean sweep of the three medals in the women's 100 metres and was so strong in the sprints that, had it been possible for a country to have four athletes in an event, and had Veronica been the fourth, it would certainly have secured the first four places (although the order in which they would have finished would be hotly debated by Jamaicans). Never in the history of athletics has a quartet of such talent been assembled for a 4x100 metres relay for women. It was, therefore, all the more regrettable that the ladies, who were expected to break the world record, did not complete the race.

As splendid as Jamaica's performance in the Beijing

Olympics was, it was only a high point and not the zenith of our possibilities. Jamaica's Beijing Summer was no more than the latest and most exciting fruits of the process of athletic development that started in 1910 with the inauguration of the Inter-scholastic Championships (CHAMPS) among Jamaica's secondary schools. Beijing was not our apotheosis. The development continues, and the single, most important factor guaranteeing further progress is the tremendous strides made in Jamaica's senior programme in athletics over the last ten years.

The triple gold medallist and world record holder, Usain Bolt, is locally trained; so too Shelly-Ann Fraser, gold medallist in the 100 metres; Sherone Simpson, silver medallist in the 100 metres; Asafa Powell, former world record holder in the 100 metres and gold medallist in the 4x100 metres relay along with Nesta Carter and Michael Frater; Melaine Walker, gold medallist in the 400 metres hurdles; Shericka Williams, silver medallist in the 400 metres; Rosemarie Whyte, bronze medallist in the 4x400 metres relay and Bobby-Gaye Wilkins

◀ Veronica Campbell-Brown celebrates her 200m victory.

who ran in the semi-finals of the 4x400 metres relay. Thus in quantitative terms, the locally-trained athletes accounted for about 70 per cent of the medals. However, in qualitative terms, with five gold medals their contribution is much higher.

The holders of the two fastest times in the world for the 100 metres, Usain Bolt and Asafa Powell, are wholly home-grown. As has been argued previously, Jamaica now has in the MVP Club, the HPTC and the G.C. Foster College, high quality institutions which are more than an adequate replacement of, or alternative to, training facilities in the USA.[25]

The plain truth is that Jamaica's athletes are better off remaining at home for their tertiary education and athletic development. This point was made recently by the retired Jamaican coach, Dennis Johnson, former 100 yards world record holder, and himself a product of the USA college system in the 1960s.[26]

The person principally responsible for the development of adult athletic training in Jamaica is Stephen Francis, who established the MVP Club in 1999. Of the locally-based athletes mentioned previously, all, except Usain Bolt, Rosemarie Whyte and Bobby-Gaye Wilkins, belong to the MVP Club.[27] Rosemarie attends the G.C. Foster College. Usain is trained by Jamaica's veteran coach, Glen Mills and Bobby-Gaye Wilkins is just out of high school.

▶ Did you know?

At the Beijing Olympic Games Jamaica won 7 of the 12 medals in the flat sprints.

>

At the 2008 Beijing Olympics, from a field of 204 countries, Jamaica, with 11 medals, placed third in the overall medal count.

Shericka Williams (2170) comes with an amazing stretch run to cop silver in the 400m in a first sub-50, 49.69 seconds just behind Great Britain's Christine Ohuruogu (1819) with favourite, Sanya Richards (3222) of USA, dipping for bronze.

Indeed, had the MVP Club been able to compete in Beijing as a country it would have placed sixth in the medal tables.

This is an accomplishment of the highest order, warranting fulsome praise. To have achieved what the Club has in the relatively short period of nine years and with the little resources at its disposal is nothing short of a miracle. And when today Stephen Francis' mind wanders back to that day in France at the World Junior Championships in 1998 when the insulting remarks of American coaches about the talent of Jamaican coaches prompted him to establish the MVP Club, he must certainly have a wry smile of satisfaction on his face.[28]

I am not against the education and training of Jamaicans abroad. But that should not stifle the growth of our own local educational and training institutions. As important a role as track scholarships to colleges in the USA have played in the development of Jamaican athletics, they nonetheless remain a factor explaining the very slow pace in the advance

▶ **Did you know?**

Glen Mills is Jamaica's veteran coach in track and field athletics. He attended Camperdown High School, which was to become known as the sprint factory of Jamaica, producing, among others, Donald Quarrie. Mills coached Raymond Stewart at Camperdown, and also a few months after he left school to represent Jamaica as a teenager at the 1984 Los Angeles Olympics, placing sixth in the 100 metres final. The outstanding performance of his charge, triple gold medallist Usain Bolt, at the Beijing Olympics confirmed his status as one of the top two sprint coaches in the world.

of adult athletic training in Jamaica up to the end of the last century. Fortunately for Jamaica, Stephen Francis saw the danger of the complacency that had been allowed to set in and the need for a structured approach to the training of our senior athletes. The Beijing Olympics marks an important step in the development of Jamaica's senior athletic programme.

In the third edition of *Jamaican Athletics: A Model for the World*, it was said that Glen Mills and Stephen Francis must certainly rank among the top five sprint coaches in the world. Following the achievements of their athletes at the Beijing Olympics, it is now clear they must rank in the top three; indeed, it would be difficult to refute a claim that they are the top two sprint coaches in the world.

Certainly, Glen Mills deserves the highest commendation for his work with Usain Bolt. It is gratifying to note that Jamaica has a coach with the technical expertise to impart to Usain the knowledge, enabling him to defy the conventional wisdom that excessive height is incompatible with the explosiveness required for world class 100 metres sprinting. In the four years Glen Mills

◀ Shericka Williams proudly displays the Jamaican flag after winning the silver medal in the women's 400m.

has been Usain's coach he has made modifications to the advantage of his charge in every aspect of his running, notably his start, his bend running and his stride pattern. Glen Mills and Usain Bolt have transformed the approach to the 100 metres sprint by very tall athletes. No longer will an athlete of 6 feet 4 inches or more be told by his coach to confine himself to the 400 metres and longer distances.

It is a measure of Stephen Francis' reputation as a coach that Germaine Mason, the Jamaican who won a silver medal for the UK, sacrificed the lottery funding to which he was entitled in the UK, so that he could return to Jamaica to be trained by Coach Francis.

And it is a measure of Glen Mills' reputation as a sprint coach that the authorities in the UK have indicated that they are considering sending their coaches and sprinters to Jamaica to have their skills upgraded by Coach Mills, "the most sought after guru in track and field".[29]

Thus the prediction made previously[30] – that any debt to the USA for "finishing" our athletes would shortly be repaid by American athletes being "finished" in Jamaica – is in the process of being fulfilled. For if the UK comes to Jamaica, can the USA be far behind? Indeed, there are already reports that at least one well-known American athlete is considering coming to Jamaica[31] It is a very rare experience for a developing country

Melaine Walker (2132) emphasizes her 2008 domina
the event by taking the gold in the 400m hurdles ev
the Beijing Olympics in a Meet Record, 52.64 second

like Jamaica, traditionally a net importer and consumer of technology, skills and know-how from developed countries, to be in a position to sell its own skills and know-how to a developed country. This serves to underscore the point that has been made repeatedly that track and field athletics in Jamaica has the potential to be developed as an industry providing services worldwide.[32]

Stephen Francis and Glen Mills must be acknowledged for what they are, national treasures, and they deserve greater recognition in Jamaica's Honours List.

Maurice Wilson, who is the coach of the G.C. Foster College, must also be commended for the resurgence of that College as an institution producing world class athletes.[33] He coached Rosemarie Whyte, who is the national 400 metres champion, and was a finalist in that event at the Beijing Games as well as a member of the 4x400 metres relay team that won the bronze medal at those Games.

▶ Did you know?

When Deon Hemmings and Melaine Walker won Olympic Gold Medals in the 400 metres hurdles in Atlanta, 1996 and Beijing, 2008, respectively, they both broke the Olympic record with times of 52.82 and 52.64 seconds, respectively.

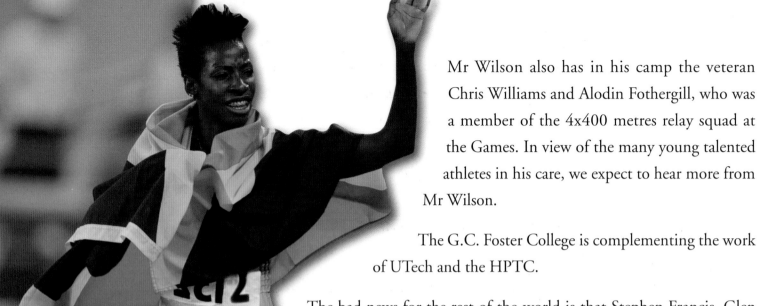

Mr Wilson also has in his camp the veteran Chris Williams and Alodin Fothergill, who was a member of the 4x400 metres relay squad at the Games. In view of the many young talented athletes in his care, we expect to hear more from Mr Wilson.

The G.C. Foster College is complementing the work of UTech and the HPTC.

The bad news for the rest-of-the-world is that Stephen Francis, Glen Mills and Maurice Wilson do not represent the totality of Jamaican coaching talent. As has been explained[34] there are deep reserves of that talent in Jamaica, where almost every secondary school has a qualified coach. This very favourable position is largely due to the transformational effect that the G.C. Foster College has had on Jamaican athletics over the last 25 years.[35] It has produced a multitude of coaches with the result that lesser known schools can produce champions and record breakers at CHAMPS.[36] An example of this phenomenon is Dexter Lee[37] of the Herbert Morrison Technical High School. In 2007 Dexter was the World Youth Champion in the 100 metres, and he is the 2008 World Junior Champion in the same event. That Herbert Morrison has been able to produce a World

◀ Melaine Walker celebrates her 400m hurdles victory.

Champion 100 metres runner in two successive years is largely due to the school's coach, Claude Grant, who is a typical example of the kind of coach coming out of the G.C. Foster College. Grant is a young man of 38 years who graduated from that College in 1998 with a Diploma and in 2005 with a Degree in Physical Education and Sport. With coaches of the ability and dedication of Claude Grant guiding young athletes, the future of Jamaican athletics is in safe hands.

An interesting feature of our achievements in Beijing is that all the locally-based medallists, except Rosemarie Whyte, are members of the UTech family. Indeed, UTech accounts for, roughly, 50 per cent of the medals won by Jamaica. The UTech and the G.C. Foster College have set a splendid example. Other tertiary educational institutions should follow by recruiting athletes out of the secondary schools. In that regard, one must note the athletic scholarships recently awarded by the University of the West Indies to students from secondary schools. The great Jamaican Olympian, Grace Jackson, is the Director of Sports at the University. These are signs that our premier tertiary educational institution is now beginning to take seriously its responsibilities in this vital area of national development. Sherone Simpson has demonstrated that athletes can also achieve great heights in the classroom. She is to be congratulated on the Upper Second Class Degree recently awarded to her by UTech. The twinning of scholarship

▶ Did you know?

Following the outstanding success of Jamaica at the Beijing Olympic Games and the confirmation of Jamaica as the sprint capital of the world, athletes in the United Kingdom and the USA are now actively considering coming to Jamaica for coaching and training at Stephen Francis' MVP Club and by Glen Mills.

The Fantastic Four: (*From left*) Asafa Powell, Nesta Carter, Usain Bolt and Michael Frater pose after their victory in the men's 4x100m final.

and athletics, of which the progenitor is no less a person than national hero, Norman Manley, is to be encouraged.

The aim of this essay is to alert Jamaicans and the world at large to the features of the environment in which the very unique and special athletic product thrives. For if you are successful, it is important to know why you have been successful, so that that knowledge can become the basis for success in the

Jamaica's Beijing Bronze Belles: (*From left*) Novelene Williams, Shericka Williams, Shereefa Lloyd and Rosemarie Whyte pose after winning the bronze medal in the women's 4x400m final.

future. We must know why there was a Herb McKenley in the 1940s and 1950s; a Lennox Miller in the 1960s; a Donald Quarrie in the 1970s; a Merlene Ottey in the 1990s; a Usain Bolt, Asafa Powell and Veronica Campbell-Brown today, so that we can be reasonably confident of reproducing athletes of that calibre.

Knowledge and its application are the basis of success in any enterprise. It is nonsense to believe that Jamaica's success is accidental, fortuitous, natural, intuitive or instinctive; it is none of those, rather, it is the result of a system that has been carefully elaborated by Jamaicans for Jamaica over the past 100 years, but whose features are, for the most part, exportable to, and capable of replication in other countries, particularly developing countries. It has been the result of an extraordinary process of evolution, calculation, planning and execution by an extraordinary group of actors who, despite niggling differences at times, have always ultimately been able to locate the solidarity that is the natural outcome of respect for Jamaica's rich legacy in athletics and the wider national interests. The notion in some quarters that Jamaica's success in global athletics has had little to do with the application of Jamaican thought and intelligence must be laid to rest.

Funding is critically important. Track and field athletics should receive funding commensurate with its status not only as the highest-ranking sport of international standard in Jamaica, but, arguably, as the highest-ranking enterprise of international standard in the country. It is surely inexplicable that athletics is not as well funded as our underachieving football. One can only endorse the hope of Dennis Johnson that the current achievements in athletics will serve as a wake-up call to the private sector to give to athletics the funding that its status warrants.[38] The Government and the Jamaican people as a whole also have a responsibility in this matter.

While we can be reasonably confident that the system that has evolved over the past 100 years will ensure that the Beijing success is not a nine-day wonder, complacency must not be allowed to set in; we must not take the success for granted. We must not commit the mistake made in West Indies cricket by not planning to build on our success. Every effort should be made to preserve and enhance the features of the system that underpin Jamaica's success in global athletics.

After six decades of truly outstanding accomplishments by our athletes, it is timely to consider the best way for the country to recognize the contribution of track and field athletics to national development. It has previously been suggested that a museum should be established to celebrate the achievements not only of our great athletes, but also the coaches and administrators.[39] This museum would be a worthy tribute to Jamaican track and field athletics, which is by far the highest quality sport of international standard. The temptation to have a multi-sport museum should be resisted. Track and field athletics has

Asafa Powell finishing the 4x100m relay, Jamaica's anchor. Asafa Powell, dips into history – first ever Olympic men's sprint relay gold with a world record 37.10.

brought more glory and fame to Jamaica than any other sport, and deserves to have a museum exclusively devoted to its achievements. Such a museum would also be a welcome boost to the tourism product.

How would such a museum be funded? If every Jamaican in the diaspora, whose spirit was lifted by the achievements of our athletes and whose head was swollen with pride every time a non-Jamaican congratulated him or her on our team's performance, contributed US$100 and if every Jamaican resident in Jamaica who was similarly moved by the Beijing events contributed a minimum of J$100, there would then be enough funds, not only for the museum, but also for the establishment of a special fund for the welfare of the athletes, past and present, and for the glory of Jamaica, Land we love.

II. *Conclusion*

I CONCLUDE BY RETURNING TO THE SYSTEM. Nothing in what I have said about its excellence is to be taken as meaning that it is perfect. It has many of the problems that affect organizations, whether in Jamaica or elsewhere. I have already referred to the lack of funds. The system deserves more support, and as good as it is, it would be better with additional support. It is not without internecine struggles. But despite these problems and more, it is still successful; it is almost as though the system has reached a stage in its development where it is capable of driving itself. The success is the more remarkable when one considers that many of the participants in the system are in fact volunteers, who derive no income from athletics.

What this book has sought to do is to isolate the environment in which the Jamaican athletic product of excellence thrives. This environment consists of the rich legacy and history of athletics in Jamaica, the innate competitive, assertive and resilient spirit characteristic of Jamaicans, the athletic talent that abounds in Jamaica, and the systemic and structural features that underpin the junior and senior athletic programmes.

▶ Did you know?

In her eight years of competition at the highest level of global athletics Veronica Campbell-Brown has won medals that in quantity and quality, surpass those won by any other Jamaican.

1) 2000 Sydney Olympics – Silver 4x100 metres relay.

2) 2004 Athens Olmypics – Gold 200 metres; Gold 4x100 metres relay and Bronze 100 metres.

3) 2008 Beijing Olympics – Gold 200 metres.

4) 2005 Helsinki World Championships – Silver 100 metres and Silver 4x100 metres relay.

5) 2007 Osaka World Championships – Gold 100 metres; Silver 200 metres and Silver 4x100 metres relay.

Total of ten medals, comprised of 4 gold, 5 silver and 1 bronze.

Many local and regional enterprises would benefit from some of the practices in the Jamaican athletic system. This includes the beleaguered West Indies cricket team. It is not for nothing that the former Prime Minister of Grenada, the Honourable Keith Mitchell, at the 46th National Sportsman and Sportswoman Awards, 2006, held in Kingston, Jamaica, February 1, 2007, said that West Indies cricket should be doing what athletics in Jamaica is doing.

Mention of cricket will bring to mind other examples of the small Caribbean countries punching above their weight on the international plane. For 20 years the West Indies cricket team, comprised of players from a group of Commonwealth Caribbean countries with a combined population of no more than five million people, dominated world cricket. There was also a time when a cricket team from Barbados, a country with less than 300,000 people in an area of 166 square miles, was capable of taking on a Rest-of-the-World team and winning. Indeed, on a per capita basis, Barbados has produced the greatest cricketers in the world. In track and field athletics itself, The Bahamas, a country with a population of 300,000, has performed superbly in global athletics over the last 15 years, placing ninth in the medal tables at the 2007 Osaka World Championships. In fact, by virtue of its very small population, the two medals won by The Bahamas in Beijing placed it at the top of the tables, on a per capita basis, with Jamaica in second place. But the greatest achievement by a Caribbean country, and one that must rank higher than

Jamaica's standing in global athletics, is that of a country not much bigger than the smallest parish in Jamaica. On two occasions Saint Lucia, a country that is 238 square miles, with a population of 160,000, has produced Nobel Laureates – Sir Arthur Lewis for Economics and Dereck Walcott for Poetry. For that matter, Trinidad and Tobago has also produced a Nobel Laureate in Sir Vidia Naipaul.

Thus, as magnificent as Jamaica's performance in international athletics is, it is but a part of a tradition of regional triumphs on the world stage by a group of small, but proud countries with whom Jamaica shares a common history of colonization, struggle and independence.

The lesson that Jamaica's achievements in athletics teaches is that smallness in size is no barrier to success at the international level, so long as the necessary talent, opportunity and will is present. And it is just as well that small countries put themselves in a position to compete at the international level, because in the modern global economy not much allowance is made for their limitation in size.

In Jamaica there is a saying that captures very neatly the contradiction, more apparent than real, between smallness and greatness. We say a person is little but "tallawah". This means that a person is small but strong. In global athletics Jamaica is little but "tallawah".

> ## Did you know?

In 2006 Jamaica produced the World Male Athlete of the Year – Asafa Powell, former World Record holder in the 100 metres, and also the world number one ranked female athlete in both the 100 and 200 metres – Sherone Simpson. Both were trained in Kingston, Jamaica by Stephen Francis of the MVP Club.

To celebrate the rich tradition in athletics, the proposal made earlier is repeated – the Jamaican authorities should establish a museum dedicated to the past and present achievements of our athletes, their coaches and administrators.

Despite the attempt I have made to identify the features that contribute to Jamaica's success in track and field athletics, the best explanation of the outstanding achievements of the system is that all of its actors are moved by a spirit that unifies them to work to ensure that Jamaican athletics lives up to its rich history and tradition of excellence. The differences that exist between some of the actors in the Jamaican athletic system do not, in my view, derogate from the fundamental spirit of unity and solidarity that runs through the system as a whole. These are differences that one would expect to find in any organization, especially one as loosely structured as the Jamaican athletic system.

The history and tradition in Jamaican athletics have over the years fostered the growth of a community of interest among the several actors in the system. It is this sense of community and solidarity, which, sadly, is missing in so many other areas of national life.

Jamaica has some of the most talented athletes in the world; we also have some of the best coaches in the world, and the Jamaican athletic system is second to none in producing world class athletes. What should Jamaica do with such world class assets? Should Jamaica sit back and relax? No. Jamaica must do what any prudent entrepreneur would. Jamaica must build on those assets, maximizing its profits.

And so I see Jamaica not only continuing the tradition of winning gold, silver and bronze medals. I see Jamaica seizing the opportunity to develop and promote those assets as an industry providing services not only to the Caribbean, but to the entire world. In short, I see a tremendous opportunity for Jamaica to become a hub for athletic services, a global athletic centre. Let those with the know-how, the wherewithal and the authority set about this task.

▶ Did you know?

Shelly-Ann Fraser is the first Jamaican to win the 100m title at the Olympics, a feat that not even the great Merlene Ottey accomplished. At the Jamaican Olympic Trials in June 2008, she clocked 10.85 seconds to place second. In Beijing she improved on that time by 0.07 seconds. Her gold medal run of 10.78 seconds makes her the second fastest Jamaican over the 100m, bettered only by Merlene Ottey's 10.74 seconds.

Annex I: Athletes with Jamaican connection by birth or descent, who have represented other countries

- **Donovan Bailey** Born in Jamaica. 1996 Olympics 100 metres Champion in world record time – 9.84 seconds for Canada.

- **Ato Boldon** Mother is Jamaican. Olympic Silver and triple Bronze Medallist; 200 metres World Champion in 1997.

- **Mark Boswell** Born in Jamaica. High jumper for Canada who won World Championships Silver and Bronze Medals (1999 and 2003 respectively).

- **Dwain Chambers** His father is Jamaican. His time of 9.87 seconds makes him the coholder with Linford Christie of the fastest British time over 100 metres.

- **Linford Christie** Born in Jamaica. 1992 Olympic 100 metres Champion for Britain, and 1988 Olympic Bronze Medallist in the 100 metres.

- **Charmaine Crooks** Born in Jamaica. Member of the Canadian Silver Medal winning 4x400 metres team in the 1984 Olympics.

- **Robert Esmie** Born in Jamaica. Sprint relay runner for Canada. Ran the first leg for Canada's 1996 4x100 metres Gold Medal team.

- **Sandra Farmer-Patrick** Born in Jamaica. Competed for Jamaica in the 1984 Olympics. Switched allegiance to the US prior to the 1988 Olympics. Olympic Silver and World Championship, Silver Medals in 1992 and 1993 respectively.

- **Olusoji Fasuba** 100 metres runner for Nigeria. Personal record is 9.85 seconds. His mother was born in Jamaica and is a cousin of Donald Quarrie.

- Kelly Holmes Father is Jamaican. Winner of the 800 metres and 1,500 metres at the Athens Olympics 2004. Only the third woman in Olympic history to accomplish this feat.

- Colin Jackson His parents are Jamaican. One time world record holder in the 110 metres hurdles. His record stood for 11 years, 7 days, was equalled by Liu Xiang of China, then broken 2 years later by Xiang. Two time World Champion, Olympic Silver Medallist in 1988 Olympics.

- Ben Johnson Born in Jamaica. 1988 Olympic Champion for Canada, 100 metres.

- Mark Lewis-Francis Parents are from Jamaica. Anchor leg runner for British 4x100 metres Gold Medal team in Athens 2004. 2000 World Junior 100 metres Champion.

- Atlee Mahorn Born in Jamaica. Ran 200 metres for Canada. 1986 Commonwealth Games Champion, and 1991 World Championships Bronze Medallist.

- Inger Miller Daughter of the great Lennox Miller. World Champion in 200 metres in 1999; Olympic Gold on the US 4x100 metres relay team in 1996.

- Cydonie Mothersill Born in Jamaica. Runs 200 metres for Cayman; 2005 Central American and Caribbean Gold Medallist in the 200 metres.

- Milt Ottey Born in Jamaica. High jumper competing for Canada. Double Commonwealth Games Champion, 1982 and 1986. Sixth place in the 1984 Olympics.

- Suziann Reid Born in Jamaica. Quarter miler competing for the US.

- Sanya Richards Born in Jamaica. Attended Vaz Prep. Number 1 ranked quarter miler in the world.

- Tessa Sanderson Born in Jamaica. 1984 Olympic Champion for Britain in the Javelin.

- Tony Sharpe Born in Jamaica. Sprinter for Canada. Member of Canada's Bronze Medal winning 4x100 metres team in the 1984 Olympic Games.

- **Diane Smith** Born in Jamaica. 200 metres runner for Britain, and World Junior Champion in 1990 in the 200 metres.

- **Kareem Streete-Thompson** Father is Jamaican. Sprinter/Long Jumper for the US and Cayman. Personal bests are: Long Jump: 28-3.75 (1994); 100 metres – 9.96 (1997)

- **Angella Taylor-Issajenko** Born in Jamaica. Sprinter who competed for Canada, Commonwealth 100 metres Champion in 1982, and Olympic Silver Medallist on Canada's 1984 Olympic 4x100 metres relay team.

- **Robert Weir** Born in England of Jamaican parents – holds what must be a unique record – Gold Medallist in two different events at the Commonwealth Games 16 years apart – the hammer in 1982 and the discus in 1995.

- **Kelli White** double World Champion from the 2003 Games. Mother is Debbie Byfield who represented Jamaica in the Munich 1972 Olympic Games.

- **Jerome Young** Born in Jamaica. Olympic Gold Medallist on US 4x400 metres team in Sydney 2000.

Annex II: The Great Trelawny Athletes

Male

- Usain Bolt – world record holder in the 100 metres and 200 metres 2008 Beijing Olympics.

- Michael Frater – in the absence of clubmate Asafa Powell he showed determination to place a surprising second for silver at the 2005 Helsinki World Championships.

- George Kerr – following the tradition set by Arthur Wint in the 800 metres, he won a bronze medal at the 1960 Rome Olympics and was fourth in the 1964 Tokyo Olympics. He was also a bronze medallist in the 4x400 metres relay in Rome.

- Marvin Anderson – he was champion boy at Boys' CHAMPS 2001 and silver medallist at the 2007 Osaka World Championship in the 4x100 metres relay.

- Lindel Frater – older brother of Michael, he made the 1996 Atlanta Olympic team while still a school boy, and ran the opening leg on the sprint relay team at the 2000 Sydney Olympics, Jamaica finishing in fourth place.

- Omar Brown – husband of Veronica Campbell, severely hampered by recurring injury; he is the 200 metres Commonwealth gold medallist (2006 Melbourne) and holds World Youth Championship medals for both sprints (bronze in the 100 metres and silver in the 200 metres) from the inaugural staged in Bydgoszcz, 1999.

- Ben Johnson – represented Canada in the 100 metres.

- Ricardo Chambers – semi-finalist in the 400 metres at the Beijing Olympic Games.

Annex II: The Great Trelawny Athletes *(cont'd)*

Female

- Veronica Campbell-Brown – has won a plethora of high quality medals at the Olympic Games, the World Championships and the Commonwealth Games. Her medals include gold at the 2004 Athens Olympics in the 200 metres and the 4x100 metres relay, and gold at the 2007 Osaka World Championships in the 100 metres.

- Debbie-Ann Paris – represented Jamaica with distinction in the 400 metres hurdles, placing fourth at the 1996 Atlanta Olympics. Paris was a member of Jamaica's gold medal 4x400 metres relay team at the 2001 Edmonton World Championships.

- Audrey Reid – represented Jamaica in the high jump at the 1968 Mexico City Olympics, the 1972 Munich Olympics and the 1976 Montreal Olympics. She was the 1971 Central American and Caribbean Champion, and silver medallist in the 1971 Pan American Games.

- Dorothy Scott – represented Jamaica in the long jump at the Olympic Games in Moscow 1980 and Los Angeles 1984, making the final in the latter.

- The Turner sisters. Inez, Janice and Evette – out of a traditionally productive Vere Technical School middle/long distance programme, under coach, Constantine "Consie" Haughton, between them, they won nine national senior titles (Inez, 800m – '91, '92, '95, '97) (Janice 1500m – '91, '93, '94) and Evette, the youngest, (3000m – '91 & '92). Inez, the 800 metres Commonwealth Champion (Victoria '94), was back to back NCAA Outdoor Champion ('94, '95) and Pan Am Junior Champion (Kingston '91); she was forced to run the 400 metres to make national teams. Janice was Pan Am Junior 1500m bronze medallist (Kingston '91). Evette's time of 4:22.30 in the 1500 metres at the 1992 Seoul World Junior Championships is the National Junior Record.

- Astia Walker – represented Jamaica at the 1994 World Junior Championships, when she reached the final in both the 200 metres and the 100 metres hurdles; member of the Jamaica team to the 1996 Atlanta Olympics, World Championships in Athens, 1997 and Edmonton, 2001.

- Vernicha James – represented the United Kingdom at the 2002 World Junior Championships, where she won the gold medal in the 200 metres, ahead of Jamaica's Anneisha Mclaughlin.

- Rosemarie Whyte – national 400 metres champion in 2008, finalist in that event and bronze medallist in the 4x400 metres relay at the Beijing Olympic Games.

Annex III: Preview of the Beijing Olympics, Medals Won and Finalists in Beijing

It is well established that the standard of Jamaican athletics is much higher than that of many bigger and much better resourced countries. The gap between Jamaica and those countries in achievements and the expectations to which they give rise is illustrated in an article captioned "Tomlinson upbeat on Great Britain medal haul".[40] The article refers to the target of 5 medals in the forthcoming Beijing Olympic Games set by Dave Collins, the UK Athletics Performance Director.

A conservative preview is that Jamaica could win between 8 and 11 medals, of which 4 or 5 might be gold; a less conservative outlook shows Jamaica winning a possible 17 medals.

Jamaica should certainly aim to win at least as many as the 10 medals it won at the 2007 Osaka World Championships.

The preview below of Jamaica's prospects assumes the good health of the athletes and reasonably good baton changes in the relays.

A conservative estimate shows Jamaica winning medals in the following events:

WOMEN

100 metres (1 or 2)

200 metres (1 or 2)

4x100 metres (1)

400 metres (1)

4x400 metres (1)

A total of 5 to 7 medals, 2 of which might be gold

MEN

100 metres (1 or 2)

200 metres (1)

4x100 metres (1)

A total of 3 to 4 medals, 2 or 3 of which might be gold

A less conservative estimate shows Jamaica winning medals in the following additional events:

WOMEN

100 metre hurdles (1)

400 metre hurdles (1)

800 metres (1)

A total of 3 medals (bronze)

MEN

Decathlon (1)

Shot put (1) If Dorian Scott achieves his personal record of 21.45 metres, he might win a bronze medal.

400 metre hurdles (1) – Do not count out the old lion, Danny McFarlane, silver medallist at the last Games.

A total of 3 medals

Medals Won in Beijing

MEN

1.	Usain Bolt	100 metres	Gold (WR)
2.	Usain Bolt	200 metres	Gold (WR)
3.	Nesta Carter Michael Frater Usain Bolt Asafa Powell	4x100 metres	Gold (WR)

WOMEN

1.	Shelly-Ann Fraser	100 metres	Gold
2.	Sherone Simpson	100 metres	Silver
3.	Kerron Stewart	100 metres	Silver
4.	Veronica Campbell-Brown	200 metres	Gold
5.	Kerron Stewart	200 metres	Bronze
6.	Shericka Williams	400 metres	Silver
7.	Melaine Walker	400 metres hurdles	Gold (OR)
8.	Shericka Williams Shereefa Lloyd Rosemarie Whyte Novelene Williams	4x400 metres	Bronze

FINALISTS

1.	Danny McFarlane	400 metres	4th
2.	Chelsea Hammond	Long Jump	4th

3.	Deloreen Ennis-London	100 metres hurdles	5th
4.	Brigitte Foster-Hylton	100 metres hurdles	6th
5.	Michael Blackwood Ricardo Chambers Sanjay Ayre Lansford Spence	4x400 metres relay	8th
6.	Markino Buckley	400 metres hurdles	7th
7.	Maurice Wignall	110 metres hurdles	6th
8.	Richard Phillips	110 metres hurdles	7th
9.	Kenia Sinclair	800 metres	6th
10.	Rosemarie Whyte	400 metres	7th
11.	Shelly-Ann Fraser Sherone Simpson Kerron Stewart Veronica Campbell-Brown	4x100 metres relay	Did Not Finish
12.	Maurice Smith	Decathlon	9th
13.	Trecia-Kaye Smith	Triple Jump	11th
14	Asafa Powell	100 metres	5th
15	Michael Frater	100 metres	6th

Forty-three Jamaicans actually participated in track and field athletics in Beijing. Jamaica won 11 medals including 6 gold. Counting a relay team as a single unit and including the medallists who reached the final of events in which they did not medal, Jamaica had 15 finalists other than medallists. By any manner of reckoning this is an outstanding statistic that speaks volumes not only about the depth of the team's quality, but also the strength of the pool from which the team was drawn and the efficacy of the selection process.

Annex IV: Boys' Champs Records

Event	Name	School	Mark	Date
CLASS I (UNDER 19 YEARS*)				
100m	Yohan Blake	St Jago High	10.21	2007
200m	Usain Bolt	William Knibb	20.25	2003
400m	Usain Bolt	William Knibb	45.35	2003
800m	Sherwin Burgess	Vere Technical	1:48.94	1987
1500m	Dudley Dawkins	Vere Technical	3:51.97	1992
110m Hurdles 39"	Keiron Stewart	Kingston College	13.53	2007
4x100m		St Jago High	39.78	2008
High Jump	Enrico Gordon	Wolmer's Boys	2.15m	1995
Long Jump	Leon Gordon	Vere Technical	7.87m	1993
Shot Put 6 kg.	Camoi Hood	Bridgeport High	16.70m	2005
Discus 1.75 kg.	Camoi Hood	Bridgeport High	51.05m	2005
CLASS II (UNDER 16 YEARS*)				
100m	Yohan Blake	St Jago High	10.34	2006
200m	Ramone McKenzie	Calabar High	20.89	2007
400m	Ramone McKenzie	Calabar High	47.24	2007
800m	Aldwyn Sappleton	Edwin Allen	1:52.27	1997
1500m	Kemoy Campbell	Bellfield High	3:58.06	2007
110m Hurdles 36"	Warren Weir	Calabar High	13.92	2006
4x100m		Calabar High	41.24	2006
High Jump	Jermaine Mason	Wolmer's Boys	2.09m	1999
Long Jump	Paul Thompson	Munro College	7.70m	1998
Shot Put 5 kg.	Sean Samuels	Calabar High	16.01m	2005
Discus 1.50 kg.	Sharif Small	Jamaica College	48.77m	2004

Annex IV continues on next page

Event	Name	School	Mark	Date
CLASS III (UNDER 14 YEARS)				
100m	Adam Cummings	Munro College	10.91	2008
200m	Travis Drummond	Calabar High	22.17	2007
400m	Ali Watson	Calabar High	49.12	1991
800m	Waqar Dacosta	Jamaica College	1:58.06	2007
100m Hurdles 33"	Mathew Palmer	Wolmer's Boys	13.11	2001
4x100m		Kingston College	43.41	2007
High Jump	Ryan Chambers	Calabar High	1.98m	1993
Long Jump	Paul Thompson	Munro College	6.97m	1996
OPEN EVENTS				
5000m	Jermaine Mitchell	St Elizabeth Technical	14:45.05	1992
400m Hurdles	Josef Robertson	Wolmer's Boys	50.24	2006
4x400m		St Jago High	3:09.51	2007
Triple Jump	Wilbert Walker	Morant Bay High	15.74m	2004
Pole Vault	Jabari Ennis	Kingston College	4.40m	1998
Heptathlon	Dwight Webley	Wolmer's Boys	4,852 points	2006
MEDLEY RELAY CLASS I AND II				
First 400 metres by a Class I Athlete, next 200 metres by a Class II Athlete, next 200 metres by a Class II Athlete, and final 800 metres by a Class I Athlete.				
		Calabar High	3:27.23	1990
		St Elizabeth Technical	3:27.23	1992

*All ages reckoned as of September 1 of the calendar year preceding CHAMPS which normally takes place in March or April.

Annex V: Girls' Champs Records

Event	Name	School	Mark	Date
CLASS I (UNDER 19 YEARS*)				
100m	Veronica Campbell	Vere Technical	11.13	2001
200m	Simone Facey	Vere Technical	22.74	2004
400m	Sonita Sutherland	Holmwood	51.13	2006
800m	Kayann Thompson	Edwin Allen	2:03.75	2004
1500m	Kayann Thompson	Edwin Allen	4.30.79	2004
100m Hurdles 26"	Astia Walker	Vere Technical	13.6	1993
4x100m		Holmwood	44.26	2004
High Jump	Peaches Roach	Alpha	1.84m	2003
Long Jump	Elva Goulbourne	Dinthill	6.47m	1998
Discus 1 kg.	Salcia Slack	Holmwood	45.13m	2008
CLASS II (UNDER 17 YEARS*)				
100m	Jura Levy	Vere Technical	11.46	2008
200m	Anneisha McLaughlin	Holmwood	23.13	2002
400m	Sonita Sutherland	Holmwood	52.41	2004
800m	Carlene Robinson	Christiana	2.07.74	2001
1500m	Evette Turner	Vere Technical	4.32.10	1993
100m Hurdles 26"	Latoya Greaves	Queen's High	13.39	2003
4x100m		Edwin Allen	45.04	2006
High Jump	Sheree Francis	Vere Technical	1.83m	2000
Long Jump	Salcia Slack	Holmwood	6.11	2007
Discus 1 kg.	Tanya Thomas	Manchester	43.42m	1996

Annex V continues on next page

Annex V: Girls' Champs Records *(cont'd)*

Event	Name	School	Mark	Date
MEDLEY RELAY CLASS I AND II				

First 400 metres by a Class I Athlete, next 200 metres by a Class II Athlete, next 200 metres by a Class II Athlete and final 800 metres by a Class 1 Athlete.

Event	Name	School	Mark	Date
		Vere Technical	4.02.41	
CLASS III (UNDER 15 YEARS)				
100m	Lisa Sharpe	Elwin Allen	11.65	1999
200m	Anneisha McLaughlin	Holmwood	23.11	2001
400m	Anneisha McLaughlin	Holmwood	52.52	2001
800m	Natoyea Goule	Manchester	2:09.6	2006
1500m	Evette Turner	Vere Technical	4:20.20	1992
80m Hurdles 26"	Kareecia Thompson	Immaculate	11.33	1996
4x100m		Holmwood	45.84m	2001
High Jump	Shelly Ann Gallimore	Meadowbrook	1.74m	1997
	Shanice Hall	Wolmer's Girls	1.74m	2008
	Peta-Gaye Reid	STETHS	1.74m	2008
Long Jump	Sheree Frances	Vere Technical	5.99m	1999
Discus 1 kg.	Peta-Gaye Beckford	Holmwood	38.70m	2000
CLASS IV (UNDER 13 YEARS)				
100m	Denesha Morris	Manchester	11.93	2004
2000m	Diane Dietrich	Immaculate	24.70	1999
70m Hurdles 26"	Tulia Robinson	Manchester	10.50	1993
Long Jump	Opal James	STETHS	5.52m	2008
High Jump	Anna Kaye Campbell	St Andrew	1.63m	1999
4x100m		Manchester	48.02	2005

Annex V continues on next page

Annex V: Girls' Champs Records *(cont'd)*

Event	Name	School	Mark	Date
OPEN EVENTS				
400m Hurdles 26"	Melaine Walker	St Jago High	56.55	2001
3000m	Evette Turner	Vere Technical	9.48.06	1992
4x400m		Holmwood	3:35.28	2006
Triple Jump	Kimberly Williams	Vere Technical	13.52m	2007
Shot Put 4 kg.	Micara Vassell	St Hughs	12.80m	2008
Javelin 600 grms.	Tamesha Blair	Holmwood	47.85m	2007
Heptathlon	Salcia Slack	Holmwood	5,411 points	2008

*All ages reckoned as of September 1 of the calendar year preceding CHAMPS which normally takes place in March or April.

Annex VI: National Junior Records – Male

Event	Mark	Name	Venue	Date
100m	10.11 w* 1.2	Yohan Blake	Providenciales	April 7, 2007
200m	19.93 w* 1.4 WJR**	Usain Bolt	Hamilton	April 11, 2004
400m	45.21	Davian Clarke	Kingston	June 24, 1995
800m	1:46.6	Neville Myton	Kingston	August 15, 1964
1500m	3:42.57	Kemoy Campbell	New York	June 8, 2008
5000m	15:03.9	Preston Campbell	Kingston	April 1, 1993
3000 Steeplechase	9:37.21	Preston Campbell	Kingston	March 20, 1993
110m Hurdles	13.49 w* 0.2	Kerion Stewart	Providenciales	April 9, 2007
400m Hurdles	50.24	Josef Robertson	Kingston	March 31, 2006
High Jump	2.27	Jermaine Mason	Kingston	June 20, 2002
Pole Vault	4.60	Jabari Ennis	Tampa	July 11, 1999
Long Jump	8.13	James Beckford	Odessa	May 20, 1994
Triple Jump	1.3 17.29 w*	James Beckford	Tempe	April 2, 1994
Shot Put	18.40	Kimani Kirton	Spanish Town	March 1, 2003
Discus	52.79	Sharif Small	Port-of-Spain	July 16, 2006
Javelin	60.50	Hubert Knight	Kingston	March 13, 1993
Decathlon	6,996 points	Maurice Smith	Tampa	July 10, 1999
	11.22, 6.79, 12.75, 1.94, 50.65, ... 15.68, 43.19, 3.05, 52.68, 4:30.97			
RELAYS				
4x100m	39.05	Team Jamaica	Beijing	August 20, 2006
	Winston Barnes, Remaldo Rose, Cawayne Jervis, Yohan Blake			
4x400m	3:04.06	Team Jamaica	Kingston	July 21, 2002
	Sekou Clarke, Usain Bolt, Jermaine Myres, Jermaine Gonzales			

* Wind speed
** World Junior Record

Annex VII: National Junior Records – Female

Event	Mark	Name	Venue	Date
100m	11.12 w* 2.0	Veronica Campbell	Santiago	October 18, 2000
200m	22.71 w* 0.7	Simone Facey	Kingston	March 27, 2004
400m	50.92	Sandie Richards	Odessa	May 10, 1987
800m	2:02.67	Kayann Thompson	Grosseto	July 16, 2004
1500m	4:22.30	Evette Turner	Seoul	September 8, 1992
3000m	9:31.5	Evette Turner	Kingston	July 3, 1992
100m Hurdles	13.07 w* 1.1	Gillian Russell	Kingston	July 3, 1992
400m Hurdles	55.11	Kaliese Spencer	Beijing	August 17, 2006
High Jump	1.87	Peaches Roach	Spanish Town	June 14, 2003
Long Jump	6.53 w* 0.9	Nolle Graham	Durham	June 1, 2000
Triple Jump	13.75 w* 0.8	Shelly-Ann Gallimore	Baton Rouge	May 14, 2000
Shot Put	15.29	Zara Northover	Durham	May 10, 2003
Discus	47.44	Melissa Gibbons	Kingston	June 19, 1999
Discus	48.19 **	Latanya Nation	Kirkvine	February 22, 2006
Javelin	47.85	Tanesha Blair	Kingston	March 30, 2007
Heptathlon	5,411 points***	Salcia Slack	Holmwood	March 2008
RELAYS				
4x100m	43.40	Team Jamaica	Kingston	July 21, 2002
Sherone Simpson, Kerron Stewart, Anneisha McLaughlyn, Simone Facey				
4x400m	3:29.66	Team Jamaica	Philadelphia	April 26, 2001
Kerron Stewart, Sheryl Morgan, Melaine Walker, Patricia Hall				

* Wind speed

**This mark was done outside of a stadium setting, on the Kirkvine Sports Club grounds at the 2006 Central Championships.

*** Lacena Golding scored 5,385 points in Austin, Texas on April 7, 1994. Event details cannot be located.

Annex VIII: National Records – Male

Event	Mark	Name	Venue	Date
100m	9.69 w1.8	Usain Bolt	Beijing	August 16, 2008
200m	19.30	Usain Bolt	Beijing	August 20, 2008
400m	44.49	Roxbert Martin	Kingston	June 21, 1997
800m	1:45.21	Seymour Newman	Helsinki	June 29, 1977
1500m	3:39.19	Steve Green	Victoria	August 28, 1994
3000m	7:55.78	Mark Elliot	Luzern	June 24, 1989
5000m	13:33.10	Mark Elliot	Koblenz	August 23, 1989
10000m	28:32.44	Mark Elliot	Arhus	July 6, 1989
3000 Steeplechase	8:52.82	Lionel Scott	Indianapolis	May 4, 1985
110m Hurdles	13.17 w0.1	Maurice Wignall	Athens	August 26, 2004
400m Hurdles	47.60	Winthrop Graham	Zurich	August 4, 1993
Marathon	2:16:39.00	Derrick Adamson	Philadelphia	November 25, 1984
High Jump	2.34	Jermaine Mason	Santo Domingo	August 9, 2003
Long Jump	8.62 w0.7	James Beckford	Orlando	April 5, 1997
Pole Vault	5.30	Jabari Ennis	Coral Gable	March 16, 2002
Triple Jump	17.92 w1.9	James Beckford	Odessa	May 20, 1995
Shot Put	21.45	Dorian Scott	Florida	March 28, 2008
Discus	62.10	Kevin Brown	Ipswich	August 3, 2000
Javelin	68.97	Robert Barnes	Kingston	June 21, 2003
Hammer	61.48	Nigel Green	Baton Rogue	May 11, 1996
Decathlon	8,349 points	Maurice Smith	Ratingen	June 24–25, 2006
10.69/w-0.8, 7.51/w1.8, 16.07, 1.91, 48.36, 14.00/w-0.1, 48.90, 4.55, 55.54, 4:30.62				
Race Walk 20km	1:40.11	Byron Williams	Brighton	April 15, 1972
4x100m	37.14	Team Jamaica	Beijing	August 22, 2008
Nesta Carter, Michael Frater, Usain Bolt, Asafa Powell				
4x400m	2:56.75	Team Jamaica	Athens	August 10, 1997
Danny McFarlane, Michael McDonald, Davian Clarke, Greg Haughton				

Annex IX: National Records – Female

Event	Mark	Name	Venue	Date
100m	10.74 w1.3	Merlene Ottey	Milan	September 7, 1996
200m	21.64 w0.8	Merlene Ottey	Brussels	September 13, 1991
400m	49.30	Lorraine Fenton	Monaco	July 19, 2002
800m	1:57.88	Kenia Sinclair	Rethimno	July 21, 2006
1500m	4:01.84	Yvonne Graham	Monte Carlo	July 25, 1995
3000m	8:37.07	Yvonne Graham	Zurich	August 16, 1995
5000m	15:07.91	Yvonne Graham	Berlin	September 1, 1995
3000m Steeplechase	9:27.21	Mardrea Hyman	Monaco	September 9, 2005
100m Hurdles	12.45 w0.8	Brigitte Foster	Eugene	May 24, 2003
400m Hurdles	52.64	Melaine Walker	Beijing	August 20, 2008
High Jump	1.90	Dianne Guthrie	Harrisonburgh	April 11, 1992
Long Jump	7.16A w0.1	Elva Goulbourne	Ciudad de Mexico	May 22, 2004
Triple Jump	15.16 w0.7	Trecia-Kaye Smith	Linz	August 2, 2004
Shot Put	18.28	Kim Barrett	Gainesville	May 29, 2004
Discus	53.58	Marlene Lewis	Abilene	May 15, 1986
Hammer	63.75	Grettel Miller-Tjiroze	Provo	July 7, 2001
Javelin	61.10	Olivia Mckoy	Nassau	July 10, 2005
Heptathlon	6527	Dianne Guthrie	Knoxville	June 3, 1995

13.86w, 1.86, 13.80, 24.91, 6.92w, 49.04, 2:20.82

RELAYS				
4x100m	41.73	Team Jamaica	Athens	August 27, 2004

Tayna Lawerence, Sherone Simpson, Aleen Bailey, Veronica Campbell

4x400m	3:20.65	Team Jamaica	Edmonton	August 12, 2001

Sandie Richards, Catherine Scott, Debbie Parris, Lorraine Fenton

Notes

1. Count Rogge's sentiments are similar to those expressed earlier by the author in a letter to the Jamaican *Daily Gleaner* in the first part of 2006, shortly after the Jamaican Government's announcement of its National Honorees for the year. The letter congratulated the honorees from the field of athletics: Teddy McCook, Neville Myton, Clement Radcliffe and Stephen Francis. In that letter it was said that "Jamaica's success in track and field athletics is not an accident; it is the result of a system of management and administration that has been in place, tested over many years, and is now well established." The letter, which was not published in the local edition of the newspaper, was subsequently published in the overseas UK edition, the *Voice*, on January 15–21 and 22–28, 2007.

2. Quite apart from this impressive list of athletes, there is a staggeringly long list of outstanding athletes who have represented other countries, and who have a connection with Jamaica by birth or descent. This list is set out in Annex I.

3. Edward Seaga, 'The Folk Roots of Jamaican Cultural Identity' (Inaugural Lecture, The University of the West Indies, May 12, 2005), pp 10 & 11.

4. See Stokeley Marshall, 'Inner City Triumph in Beijing', Jamaica *Sunday Herald*, August 24, 2008.

5. See Claire Forrester's excellent description of Cameron's feat in *World Beaters* edited by Fitzroy Nation (Kingston, Jamaica: JP Publications Ltd), p 53.

6. Patrick Cooper, *Black Superman: A Cultural and Biological History of the People Who Became the World's Greatest Athletes* (First Sahara Enterprises, 2004).

7. RA Scott, YP Pitsiladis, 'Genetics and the success of east Africa distance runners', *International SportMed Journal* vol. 7, no. 3 (2006): 172–86.

8. N Yang, DG MacArthur, B. Wolde, VO Onywera, MK Boit, SY Mary-Ann Lau, RH Wilson, RA Scott, YP Pitsiladis, Kathryn North, 'The ACTN3 R%77X polymorphism in East and West African athletes', *Medicine & Science in Sports & Exercise* vol. 39, no. 11(2007): 1985–88; see also Errol Morrison and Patrick Cooper 'Some Biomedical Mechanisms in Athletic Prowess', *West Indian Medical Journal* vol. 5, no. 3 (2006): 205.

9. Supra note 3, p 19 citing Sally Grantham-McGregor and WA Hanke, 'Developmental Assessment of Jamaican Infants', *Developmental Medical Child Neurology* vol. 13 (1971): 582–89.

10. *Jamaican Athletics: A Model for the World*, written and published by Patrick Robinson, (Kingston, Jamaica: March 2007, July 2007 and July 2008).

11. Sophie Tutkovis, 'On Paradise Island: In quest of the secrets of Jamaican sprint', *L'Equipe Magazine* No. 1293 (April 14, 2007). Unofficial translation of the French original text. Muriel Hurtis (a French athlete and many time medallist at the elite level) and Reina-Flor Okari, together with their trainer Jacques Piasenta, spent ten days in Jamaica. A tour and learning experience following the tracks of Asafa Powell, the world's fastest man.

12. In the earlier era, the legendary G.C. Foster coached four different schools to victory at CHAMPS: Calabar High School, Jamaica College, Kingston College and Wolmer's Boys School.

13. Jamaican dialect for "here".

14. Michael Manley, 'Sir Frank Worrell, Cricket and West Indies Society', in *An Area of Conquest: Popular Democracy and West Indies Cricket Supremacy*, ed. Hilary Beckles (Kingston: Ian Randle Publishers, 1994), pp 146–47.

15. Reported in an article by Kwame Lawrence, 'The MVP prototype: T & T elite training possible in T & T', *Trinidad Express,* June 20, 2008.

16. Professor Trevor Munroe, guest speaker at the launch of the book *Jamaican Athletics: A Model for the World*, Kingston, Jamaica, March 24, 2007.

17. Ibid.

18. Jamaican dialect for 'Jamaica' or 'at home'.

19. The famous exhortation of Jamaica's National Hero, Marcus Garvey: "Up you mighty race! You can accomplish what you will".

20. Cited in an article captioned "Mason tells rivals to jump to it: High-jumper Germaine Mason wins medals for GB but trains in Jamaica", by Richard Lewis, *Sunday Times*, August 31, 2008.

21. Supra note 10; first edition p 28; second edition, p 60; third edition, p 92.

22. Supra note 4.

23. Article captioned, "Good came from the ghetto – Fraser's mom". *The Gleaner*, August 28, 2008 – taken from www.chinadaily.com.cm

24. See Annex III, Preview of the Beijing Olympics.

25. Supra note 10, First edition, p 26; Second edition p 54; and Third edition, p 75.

26. See Howard Campbell, 'Home Sweet Home: Jamaican-based training spares athletes' drug taint', Jamaica *Gleaner,* Sunday, August 24, 2008.

27. For a discussion of the Senior Programme, see chapter 'Features of the System: Senior Level', third edition, pp 62–75 and supra pp 62–74.

28. Ibid., third edition, pp 70, 71 and supra p 70.

29. Michael Phillips, 'British Prepare to go to Jamaica and Bolt's Guru to Build Success', *The Guardian*, September 2, 2008.

30. Supra note 10, First edition, p 22; Second edition, p 49; Third edition, p 68 and supra p 67.

31. See article by Anthony Foster in the *Jamaica Gleaner*, September 24, 2008 reporting that Wallace Spearmon, silver medallist in the 200 metres in Beijing, was considering coming to Jamaica for training with the MVP Club.

32. Ibid., First edition, p 28; Second edition, p 60; and Third edition, p 90 and infra p119.

33. Ibid., Third edition, p 73 and supra p 64 for the reference to Devon Morris and Danny McFarlane, past and present representatives of Jamaica respectively, who are former students of the College.

34. Ibid., First edition, p 16; Second edition, p 28, 30; and Third edition, pp 49–51 and supra pp 49–51.

35. Supra pp 49–51.

36. Supra pp 49–51.

37. 'Rising Stars', supra p 42.

38. Howard Campbell, 'Home Sweet Home: Jamaican-based training spares athletes' drug taint'.

39. See note 10, First edition, p 27; Second edition, p 59; and Third edition, p 91.

40. Sarah Holt, 'Tomlinson Upbeat on GB Medal Haul', http://news.bbc.co.uk/sport2/hi/olympics/athletics/7453751.stm.